JOB MATCHING FOR YOUTH IN ASIA AND THE PACIFIC

A TRANSITIONS APPROACH FOR POSITIVE LABOR MARKET PATHWAYS

Helen Osborne and Paul Vandenberg

NOVEMBER 2023

ASIAN DEVELOPMENT BANK

6 ADB Avenue, Mandaluyong City, 1550 Metro Manila, Philippines
Tel +63 2 8632 4444; Fax +63 2 8636 2444
www.adb.org

ISBN 978-92-9270-401-8 (print); 978-92-9270-402-5 (electronic); 978-92-9270-403-2 (ebook)
Publication Stock No. TCS230482-2
DOI: http://dx.doi.org/10.22617/TCS230482-2

Notes:
In this publication, "$" refers to United States dollars, unless otherwise specified.
ADB recognizes "China" as the "People's Republic of China," "Korea" as "Republic of Korea," and "Vietnam" as Viet Nam.

Cover design by Edith Creus.

CONTENTS

TABLES, FIGURES, AND BOXES

TABLES

FIGURES

BOXES

FOREWORD

It is an important time to be thinking about youth in the Asia and Pacific region. The aftereffects of the coronavirus disease pandemic have left young people disproportionally affected, especially in terms of their employment. This is not just about earnings—employment shocks are especially harmful for young people who are at a critical stage of personal development, social transition, and individual well-being. At the macro level, quality jobs for youth are at the center of a virtuous cycle of economic productivity and social progress. Yet the pandemic—compounded by current inflation and other pressures—has resulted in a poly-crisis, significantly disrupting the opportunities available to today's young people for earning, learning, and becoming independent. Youth from low-income and poor households are particularly vulnerable.

The current challenges, however, provide opportunities to advance innovative labor market solutions that can underpin economic, social, and human development for young people. Crosscutting quality job approaches that are fit for the future of work and inclusive of vulnerable youth are needed. This means better connections between social protection and employment policies and programs to balance the need for risk mitigation and opportunity creation for aspiring youth. It also requires bringing together relevant policy domains that shape labor supply and demand dynamics, including climate change, urbanization, digitalization, and demographic change.

Intermediation of labor supply and demand, through job matching, is a key aspect for making the labor market work efficiently, particularly in difficult economic conditions. This report is a timely contribution. It takes a considered approach to job matching, situating it in terms of the employment transitions that young people make through the labor market and connecting it into the broader youth employment support ecosystem. The report's insights have wide applicability for policymakers and practitioners designing and delivering job-matching models for youth.

This report provides a practical review of job-matching models for youth in Asia and the Pacific that can maximize knowledge sharing. It supports the broader goal of advancing research and knowledge to strengthen work on quality jobs, a key pillar of Strategy 2030. It builds on previous work by the Asian Development Bank that addresses the region's youth employment challenge and charts the way forward for governments and other stakeholders.

Wendy Walker
Director
Human and Social Development Sector Office
Sectors Group
Asian Development Bank

ACKNOWLEDGMENTS

This report was prepared as part of the work program of the Social Development Team, Human and Social Development Sector Office, Sectors Group (SG-HSD), Asian Development Bank (ADB). It was researched and written by Helen Osborne, SG-HSD consultant, and Paul Vandenberg, principal economist, Economic Research and Development Impact Department. The work was funded under (1) Support to the Implementation of Strategy 2030 Operational Plans (TA-6574), which includes, within its aims, the closing of knowledge gaps related to critical development challenges that confront developing member countries, resulting from changing socioeconomic and political landscapes, demographic shifts, increased globalization, and technological change; and (2) Quality Jobs and the Future of Work (TA-6533-REG), which includes aims to strengthen the capacity of developing member countries (DMCs) to facilitate access to quality jobs, through new directions for social protection in labor markets, and effective approaches for skills development and job facilitation.

Wendy Walker, director, Social Development Team, SG-HSD, provided valuable overall direction, support, and supervision for the study. The authors are grateful for the peer review provided by ADB staff, including Ryotaro Hayashi, social sector economist, and Oleksiy (Alex) Ivaschenko, senior social protection and jobs specialist, SG-HSD; and Sameer Khatiwada, senior public management economist, Public Sector Management and Governance Sector Office.

ABBREVIATIONS

ADB	Asian Development Bank
AI	artificial intelligence
ASEEM	Aatamanirbhar Skilled Employee Employer Mapping
COVID-19	coronavirus disease
CSR	corporate social responsibility
DDU-GKY	Deen Dayal Upadhyaya Grameen Kaushalya Yojana
GDP	gross domestic product
GOYN	Global Opportunity Youth Network
ILO	International Labour Organization
NEET	not in employment, education, or training
NISE	National Intelligence for Skills, Education, Employment and Entrepreneurship
NSDC	National Skill Development Corporation
OECD	Organisation for Economic Co-operation and Development
PES	public employment service
SDG	Sustainable Development Goal
SMEs	small and medium-sized enterprises
UNICEF	United Nations Children's Fund

EXECUTIVE SUMMARY

This report presents a transitions approach to youth job matching. It shares findings from a review of selected youth job-matching models in Asia and the Pacific, underpinned by a conceptual framework that ensures that youth job matching is analyzed in terms of youth transitions and the wider youth employment facilitation ecosystem. Transitions are the varied pathways young people take into, back into, and within the labor market. The report contributes to the growing knowledge base of the Asian Development Bank (ADB) in its service of strengthening youth employment support in the region.

Securing quality employment is a key challenge for youth in Asia and the Pacific. The region's developing economies are home to over 580 million young people ages 15–29 years. Their energy, skills, and expertise are needed to power growth and innovation as economies in the region transform, grow older, and seek to address climate change. Yet over 80% of youth who work in the region do so informally, and one in four young workers are moderately or extremely poor. Working youth are often stuck in precarious, low-quality, low-paid jobs. In addition, the youth unemployment rate is persistently two to three times the adult rate in many Asian countries, and even higher in some. Growing numbers of youth are becoming discouraged, disengaging from the labor market.

Job matching is an important mechanism for facilitating young people into quality employment. It reduces the time needed for job seekers to identify vacancies and for employers to fill them. It also improves the quality of the match so that young people obtain jobs suited to their capabilities and aspirations, and employers acquire the right talent. Effective job matching can lead to better earning and employment outcomes for youth—helping boost labor productivity, and reducing job movements in the region.

Young job seekers experience several life-cycle transitions in parallel as they attempt to enter the world of work. They face a host of personal, social, and role-in-society changes and growth experiences that affect—and can hamper—their ability to secure and to retain employment. Youthhood is a formative time of life as well as an important stage in the life course. Youth experiences determine future employment and career development. Stakeholders can adopt a "youth transitions" mindset as the very foundation of thinking about support for youth. This mindset will help them design better programs that enable youth to make fluid and progressive employment transitions into quality jobs.

Placing youth into jobs is good; placing them into quality jobs is better. This helps start them on positive career pathways toward better employment outcomes. Youth support planners should recognize that many young people do not follow a simple, one-off, school-to-work transition. They may secure work but then lose employment and be bounced out of the labor market, move from school to work but also from work back into education and training, or juggle different forms of work (e.g., part-time, contract, gig, and/or entrepreneurial) with attempts to upskill and to gain experience.

Their early years often represent a zigzagging path into and around employment—not a linear one. They thus need different types of assistance depending on their current engagement with the labor market.

Against this background, this study selected 31 youth job-matching models for review, drawn from 13 Asia and Pacific economies representing all 5 subregions. The highest number of programs are from Southeast Asia. Representation from Central and West Asia and the Pacific is low, due in part to low levels of private sector matching programs in the former and the small share of formal employment in the latter. The models are divided into six categories:

A. Government Online Portal

B. Targeted Government Program

C. Commercial Digital Platform (for profit)

D. Targeted Social Impact Model

E. Digital Bootcamp

F. Multistakeholder Partnership (corporate funded)

The review of the selected models is organized according to four factors that cover the key considerations of whom a model serves, what it offers, and how it is delivered (i.e., through which stakeholders and modality). The sample of 31 models serves to highlight key practices and features of youth job matching. Many other models operate across the region and would provide further examples—it is the authors' intention that no type of leading practice or feature is excluded. This stocktaking of approaches in the region provides a platform for further research, which may include dynamic analysis of success factors and challenges underpinning performance and sustainability of different models, or more impact evaluations to address gaps in data on effectiveness.

The review showed that the range of stakeholders engaged in youth job matching in the region has expanded. The biggest change has been the establishment of private sector job-matching platforms and job placement bootcamps, which have brought dynamism and innovation to the sector. Informal matching techniques, through personal networks, will continue to be important and are being replicated within some innovative, commercial mobile phone-based products. The role of government in the market is evolving, with a trend toward aggregation of service access and data. Social entrepreneurs and nonprofit initiatives are also making a valuable contribution in reaching underserved youth.

Also, approaches to youth job matching are diversifying in the Asia and Pacific region. The dynamics shaping growth in the sector include meeting the needs of informal workers, leveraging the potential of smart technologies and addressing demand from employers for more effective ways to find and to recruit job-ready youth. Specialist providers now support specific cohorts of disadvantaged youth in some countries and areas. A particular focus group identified in the review is young people with disabilities; a sector focus is developing pathways for disadvantaged youth into digital work. Governments must recognize that youth are best served by support tailored to their specific needs. This recognition can be useful in identifying gaps in provision that are leaving some youth cohorts underserved.

The most effective models combine job matching with related job facilitation services. These services include job preparation and search as well as skills training, social networking, and post-placement activities. When job matching is linked to other services, this tends to help youth with their nonlinear transitions, reach disadvantaged youth cohorts, and strengthen matches for improved job quality. At the policy and program levels, designers and implementers need to determine where job matching fits in the wider support ecosystem for youth. Partnerships, networks, and other collaboration models can provide mechanisms for stakeholders to combine services.

The review identified 10 different design and delivery adaptations in selected models that promote a transitions approach to youth job matching. They result in youth more likely to stay in jobs, enjoy quality work experiences, and be better supported to navigate future moves. These include securing formal wage employment, linking complementary services, earning a minimum level of income, addressing skills gaps, measuring sustainability of a match, building job market capabilities, building networks with employers, providing post-placement support, and connecting the ecosystem.

Digital technologies are a major driver of expanding access. The last 10 years have witnessed a large shift to online job-matching platforms. More recently, mobile phone apps for job matching are proliferating, including those to reach communities dominated by informal employment practices. Young job seekers gain remote and convenient access to a larger and more relevant pool of jobs. Complementary support can easily be linked. Employers benefit from reaching more prospective talent as well as other recruitment services. Providers leverage scalability. Yet efforts to blend in-person and digital modalities remain important, not only to ensure inclusion of youth who lack digital connectivity but also to cater to some young job seekers who will continue to prefer and to need some offline support.

Advanced technologies are improving the quality of job matching. Machine learning and artificial intelligence are enhancing the speed and relevance of matching between job seekers and employers. These techniques make full use of data contained in vacancy postings and job seeker profiles. Less time spent on unproductive searches builds job seeker confidence and engagement and allows employers to focus on talent development. Advanced digital techniques are being adopted by many youth job-matching services, both public and private.

Youth job matching through public employment services is patchy. In the region, there are promising tendencies among governments to invest in strengthening public employment services, youth targeting, and job-matching provision, including through adoption of digital technologies. Yet, in some countries and areas, there is a lack of youth-focused programs or ineffective implementation. In some cases, this is part of a broader lack of employment services due to weak institutional capacity and a lack of resources.

Matching services for green jobs are nascent but may have great potential. As a niche market, there are few dedicated green job-matching services in the region. The only model (commercial digital platform) identified in the review did not provide complementary services and posted only a small number of jobs. Standards to classify environment-related job positions—including in non-environment industry companies—need to be further defined as the market for green jobs grows.

Targeted programs to prepare youth and connect them to quality green jobs will help increase opportunities in the green economy.

Rural services are evolving, but rural youth remain underserved. Rural-based job seekers face spatial constraints to accessing quality work, including lack of digital and transport infrastructure and labor market information. More fundamentally, there may be few formal job opportunities in rural areas. The search by employers for staff and by youth for jobs in these areas continues to rely on informal matching processes. Some governments provide satellite locations and traveling services to serve rural communities. The use of digital sites has expanded access in rural areas—for those with digital connectivity. Low-tech mobile phone solutions are more accessible than internet sites in remote locations and hold promise in responding to the needs and preferences of young informal workers in rural areas.

Looking ahead, there are promising trends to strengthen youth job matching in the region. First, key practices can be upscaled, in particular those that emphasize the quality of work—such as wage levels, time in employment, and better information sharing between employers and youth—and those that help navigate future labor market transitions, including reskilling and/or upskilling and developing social networks and professional profiles. Second, there is better understanding of the need for policy and institutional coordination to blend different types of program offerings (e.g., holistic packages and skills-based matching), both government and nongovernment stakeholder providers, and digital and nondigital delivery modalities to meet the needs of different profiles of youth. These include opening access to growth sectors for disadvantaged groups, such as low-income, disengaged youth or those with disabilities—noting the potential for growth in green job matching. Third, digital innovations such as machine learning and artificial intelligence are transforming the efficiency and relevance of job matching, bringing benefits not only to individual job seekers and employers but also the potential to orient job matching to growth industries. Leveraging digital innovations to reach underserved youth in informal employment environments, including in rural areas, will be an important area of future growth.

There are several key policy implications for policymakers. Recommendations are discussed in chapter five of the report. They include the importance of youth employment policy—and youth job matching support specifically—being rooted in a full appreciation of the dynamic nature of youth employment transitions. Job matching programs should incorporate complementary features that increase the likelihood of a good, long-term match between youth and employers and support youth to continue to chart fulfilling and productive learning-earning pathways. To maximize inclusion, stakeholders should balance and blend in-person and technology-based support to young job seekers. Greater diversity of providers requires governments to stay vigilant in identifying continued gaps in services provision, for example meeting the needs of more disadvantaged young jobseekers. Often partnerships, networks, or other collaboration models provide efficient mechanisms for stakeholders to offer easy-to-access and coordinated services. More rigorous evaluation is needed of which job-matching models are the most effective, including which work best for different cohorts of youth, and which services and delivery modalities best meet the hiring needs of employers.

132301

1 INTRODUCTION

1.1 Youth Employment Mismatch in the Region

Young people (i.e., those ages 15–29 years) in Asia and the Pacific often cannot secure quality jobs[1] despite improving participation in secondary and tertiary education. Between 2000 and 2020, lower secondary school completion rates increased from 50% to 80% in South Asia and from 77% to 92% in East Asia and the Pacific.[2] Tertiary education enrollment rates over the same time period increased in East Asia and the Pacific from under 30% to over 50% and in South Asia from 8% to 26%.[3] Yet rates of vulnerable employment among youth remain high across the region (Box 1). When the coronavirus (COVID-19) pandemic struck in 2020, more than 4 in 5 young people were working informally, often with low wages and in poor conditions, compared with about 7 in 10 adults. One-quarter of young workers lived in extreme or moderate poverty versus less than one-fifth of adults (ADB and ILO 2020).[4]

Young people's employment is disproportionately affected by socioeconomic shocks compared with that of adults. Past economic shocks show that negative effects on youth prove intractable across youth well-being, health status, and job outcomes (Bell and Blanchflower 2011).

1 Quality means decent working conditions, wages, working hours, break times, provision of job-related social security, and levels of worker satisfaction, among other factors. United Nations and International Labour Organization (ILO) statistics define youth as those ages 15–24 years unless stated otherwise. A notable exception are school-to-work transition statistics, which use ages 15–29 years. The higher upper bound allows for the reality that in some countries, young people stay in education longer and thus have later transitions into employment. The use of a numerical age-based classification should not obscure the recognition that "youth" is best understood as a stage or multiple stages of transition in a person's life cycle. See Chapter 3 for more about transitions.

2 World Bank. Lower Secondary Completion Rate, Total (% of Relevant Age Group)—East Asia and the Pacific. Open Data (accessed 28 February 2023); and World Bank. Lower Secondary Completion Rate, Total (% of Relevant Age Group)—South Asia. Open Data (accessed 28 February 2023).

3 Rates across countries vary significantly (e.g., rates are below 20% in some Pacific developing member countries). World Bank. School Enrollment, Tertiary (% Gross)—East Asia and the Pacific. Open Data (accessed 23 May 2023); and World Bank. School Enrollment, Tertiary (% Gross)—South Asia. Open Data (accessed 23 May 2023).

4 Note that extreme poverty is living on less than $1.90 per day, and moderate poverty is living on less than $3.20 per day.

Box 1

Regional Heterogeneity in Decent Work Deficits among Youth

A breakdown of decent work indicators shows relatively low rates of quality jobs for youth in Asia and the Pacific compared to other regions. There is also significant heterogeneity across subregions in Asia and the Pacific.

Regionally, Asia and the Pacific has the second-highest share of informally employed youth in the world, following Africa. In the region, and globally, a higher proportion of youth (86%) than adults (67%) work informally. Rates of informal employment overall vary considerably across countries of different stages of economic development, for example around 94% in Nepal and under 20% in Japan.

For those youth in working poverty, the rate in Asia and the Pacific is the third highest in the world, behind the Arab States and Africa. The rate varies considerably by subregion, from 45% in South Asia to 7% in East Asia.

Regarding youth not in employment, education, or training (NEET), their level in Asia and the Pacific is above nearly all other regions in the world. Prior to the coronavirus disease (COVID-19) pandemic, from 2010 to 2019, the average rate in Asia and the Pacific was 24%, slightly above the global average of 22% and second only to the Arab States. Of the region's NEET youth population in 2019, 82% were inactive nonstudents. The average in South Asia at 29% was 1.6 times the rate for Southeast Asia (18%) and 1.9 times that of the Pacific (16%). Within subregions, there is wide variation between economies. The COVID-19 pandemic pushed an additional nearly 10 million youth in the region into NEET status in 2020, with the situation worsening as the pandemic deepened, although data for 2021 onward are more limited.

Sources: ILO (2018, 2022a, 2022c), ADB and ILO (2020).

For example, rates of youth unemployment in the region did not recover to pre-crisis levels following the global financial crisis of 2008–2009 (ILO 2020a). For young people, a 10-percentage point decline in gross domestic product (GDP) translates, on average, into an 8-percentage point decline in youth employment. Furthermore, the decline is greater than that for adults, which is 6 percentage points (ILO 2021a).[5] In line with such past trends, youth employment is recovering from the pandemic more slowly than adult employment (ILO 2022a). The situation is compounded by high inflation in the early 2020s caused by the Russian invasion of Ukraine and other factors affecting energy and food prices. Indeed, a confluence of pandemic pressures have affected youth in the region—including interruptions in education and reduced labor demand in key youth employment sectors.

Many young people are becoming economically inactive. Being out of the labor force and feeling discouraged about the job search increase the difficulty of labor market reentry. Inactivity early in life limits labor market opportunities, outlook, and mobility and reduces long-term earnings and

[5] Based on analysis of 58 economies with available data from the second quarter of 2020. These comprise mainly middle- and high-income economies, including Australia; Hong Kong, China; Republic of Korea; Macau, China; New Zealand; Philippines; Taipei,China; Thailand; and Viet Nam.

well-being (ILO 2022c). Across the region, a complex picture emerges of young people moving into and out of unemployment (i.e., not working but still seeking work); inactivity (i.e., not working nor seeking work); and not in employment, education, or training (NEET). In the early phase of the pandemic (i.e., 2020, relative to 2019), inactivity rates among youth were rising more than unemployment rates in several countries (Figure 1). In the same period, NEET rates averaged across countries increased for all subregions of Asia and the Pacific (ILO 2022c). More recent data show variation in young people's state of labor market exclusion. Diagnostic work is needed to understand the causes and implications of the variation and to gain insight into young people's actual and potential labor force participation.[6]

Figure 1: Key Youth Employment Indicators in Selected Countries
(% change from 2019 to 2020)

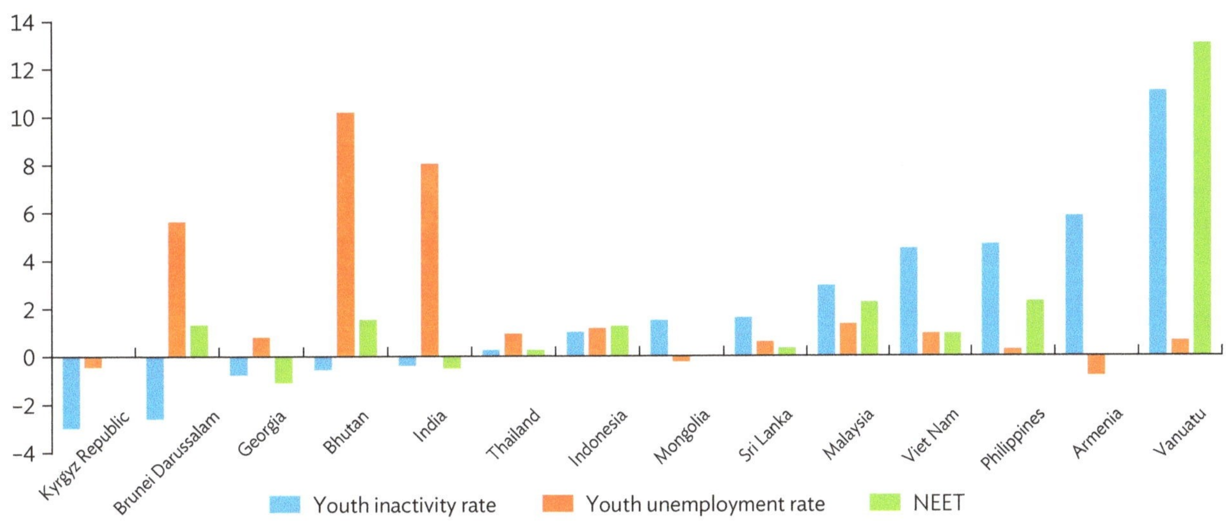

NEET = not in employment, education, or training.
Sources: ILO. Statistics on Youth. ILOStat; World Bank. World Development Indicators (both accessed June 2023).

An active young workforce underpins productivity and social progress. The labor market experiences of youth differ from those of adult workers. Young people have specific preferences and face constraints particular to their stage in life. Ensuring that they can make good first transitions into employment not only unlocks their potential but also has wider economic and social implications. Being productive and engaged from an early age can spur a virtuous cycle of economic dynamism and social progress. Young people in work can make maximum contributions to productivity both at the micro (i.e., firm) and macro levels. Quality jobs are at the core of this cycle, as recognized in global policy such as the Sustainable Development Goals (SDGs), which include a focus on youth employment (UN 2015).

6 For example, a young person may remain in the NEET category but switch from unemployment to (nonstudent) inactivity, or a young person classified as inactive may start training.

It is also recognized in Strategy 2030 of the Asian Development Bank (ADB), which states, "Favorable demographics or demographic dividends are often correlated with strong economic development and social progress, but this is contingent on the ability of [developing member countries] to offer quality jobs and [to] maximize workers' productivity" (ADB 2018b).

> **Favorable demographics or demographic dividends are often correlated with strong economic development and social progress, but this is contingent on the ability of [developing member countries] to offer quality jobs and [to] maximize workers' productivity.**
>
> — ADB (2018b)

Harnessing the potential of young people's productivity is associated with political stability and social and sustainable development. The costs of inactive youth are multiple—lower economic growth and productivity, less social inclusion and innovation, weaker community and familial ties, and less positive civic engagement (UN 2018, ILO 2022a). Indeed, unrest in various Arab States in 2011 illustrated the risks of inactive and disillusioned youth (Mulderig 2013). The COVID-19 pandemic made supporting youth's contribution to productivity more challenging. The fall-out from the pandemic—together with additional economic turbulence in the early 2020s—has hindered gains in poverty reduction in Asia and the Pacific. This can be attributed mainly to labor market causes like job losses and lack of access to social assistance (ADB 2022a).

> **Addressing the challenges of youth NEET goes beyond the issue of providing employment opportunities because it touches on education, training and skills development as well as the economic and social integration of young people.**
>
> — ILO (2022a)

Tackling the youth employment challenge requires an integrated approach. Programs and policies work best when they address the root causes and specific context of the challenge. They need to account for the three key dimensions of the labor market: labor supply, labor demand, and labor intermediation. In addition, they must do so while recognizing the complex social and well-being needs of youth, especially those who are disadvantaged (ADB 2022c). Supply-side factors determine their employability (i.e., work readiness) in terms of being prepared and qualified for quality jobs. Thus, education systems need to be dynamic and to evolve continuously to prepare young people for occupations in an ever-changing labor market (ASEAN 2021, ADB 2018a). Indeed, transforming education systems to improve employability is a global policy priority.[7]

[7] See, for example, UN. UN Transforming Education Summit.

The demand side is focused on job creation and requires that economic growth is "jobs rich," including for youth (i.e., that growth is inclusive and creates quality employment). Improving the business environment and stimulating entrepreneurship can help create employment opportunities for new labor market entrants and quality work opportunities for young workers trapped in informal, precarious, and low-quality employment (Flynn et al. 2016, Fox and Kaul 2017). Intermediation measures—including job matching—connect demand and supply, boosting the preparation of young people for work and matching them (i.e., supply) with job opportunities (i.e., demand).

Job-matching support is critical to help young people thrive in the world of work. For young people specifically, job matching is their first entry into employment as well as their onward pathway to subsequent higher-quality jobs. Understanding matching in terms of the transitions that young people make into, through, and within the labor market is central to this study. Active measures to connect youth with available employment help minimize damaging periods in which they are inactive. A focus on matching is particularly relevant to smooth the pandemic-induced disruptions to both the supply and demand sides of the labor market. Good job-matching support can lead to better earning and employment outcomes for youth if designed and implemented in a way that recognizes the complexity of the youth labor market experience. Job matching can help "rewire" a labor market to make it more efficient and inclusive for youth.

"Job matching can help "rewire" a labor market to make it more efficient and inclusive for youth.

1.2 Job Matching, Search, and Preparation

Job matching is a service that connects job seekers and employers and directly helps a job seeker secure work and an employer fill a vacancy. Job matching refers to connecting the job seeker with an employer through various services. These services are often provided in conjunction with two other types of intermediation support—job search and job preparation.[8] These may be offered by the same provider of the matching service or by a separate provider. For job search, job seekers are given assistance in looking for jobs so that matches can be made. This may include labor market information that helps them know what types of jobs are likely to be available and in demand, or travel subsidies to reach locations with better related information. Job preparation is about helping youth enter the workforce and apply for a job. These services can include career counseling, skills training and certification, job application support, and job interview preparation. Job matching, search, and preparation may be provided by governments, the private sector, civil society, and/or nonprofit organizations.

[8] Worker welfare components of intermediation (e.g., dispute resolution) are not related to job matching and are not in this report's scope.

This report provides a review and analysis of 31 job-matching models for youth in Asia and the Pacific. Analysis is set within a broader discussion of youth employment and offers considerations for policy. The report begins with an overview of job-matching theory and evidence relating to youth. Job matching is considered in terms of employment transitions for youth. It must support youth along the varied pathways they take into, back into, and within the labor market. Matching is more than a one-off transaction putting a young person into a single job. It is part of a support process that helps youth navigate transitions from one labor market state to another. These states can include moving from school to work, from inactivity into work, from one job to another job, from a low-quality job to a quality job, and from work back into training and then to work reentry. Moreover, understanding job matching as supporting employment transitions helps situate its function as one part of the broader youth employment ecosystem. Given the complexity of young people's labor market experiences, different program types are best delivered in combination as part of a connected support system and policy architecture. This lens is key to reviewing individual job-matching models properly.

Job matching is considered in terms of employment transitions for youth. It must support youth along the varied pathways they take into, back into, and within the labor market.

The report has two main objectives. The first is to deepen the understanding of the rapidly changing and wide diversity of youth job-matching mechanisms in Asia and the Pacific, while the second features recommendations for policymakers, development partners, and other stakeholders to advance effective youth job-matching policies and programs in the region. The report highlights the importance of investing in youth economic empowerment to generate inclusive and sustainable growth and advances job matching as a timely priority to mitigate the effects of socioeconomic shocks. It contributes a way of framing youth employment transitions that can underpin good design and implementation of youth employment policies and practices, including job matching.

The review is guided by four research questions. What are the different models of youth job matching in the region? How are youth job-matching services being delivered, including the latest innovations and leading practices? Where are some of the most promising practices and features of selected models? Who is leading high-performing approaches, and how are different stakeholders engaging in the youth job-matching ecosystem? In addition, issues of impact and scale are considered—however, most models reviewed in this report have not been rigorously evaluated for effectiveness by others.

Selection criteria are built from the research questions. The report does not provide a comprehensive inventory of youth job-matching interventions in the region. Instead, it draws from 31 examples (i.e., models) to illustrate key features and practices in response to the four questions.[9] Selection criteria for the examples prioritized youth targeting, stakeholder roles, geographic diversity, and ability to provide lessons and to guide replication. Models were identified based on citations in relevant literature and online searches, but a structured search protocol was not used. The job-matching market is huge; a systematic review of the totality of that market was not possible. Models without a strong web presence and documented in languages other than English were generally not included.[10] Many other models operate across the region and would provide further examples. It is the authors' intention that no types of leading practice or feature are excluded. This stocktaking of approaches in the region provides a platform for further research. For example, studying the success factors and challenges underpinning progress, over time, of different models would be valuable. This could include a case study approach that accounts for local market dynamics that influence performance and sustainability. Data on effectiveness of current models are scarce and inconsistent. Thus, more impact evaluations would also help strengthen the evidence base.

The report is structured in six chapters. Following this introduction, the second chapter outlines the role of job matching in supporting youth employment transitions. It presents recent insights from the literature into job-matching design principles and successes. The third chapter locates job matching in the broader youth employment ecosystem and provides key concepts relating to youth employment transitions. Chapter 4 then provides a review of youth job-matching models in Asia and the Pacific. It is organized along a typology of models in the region and highlights key practices and features of the various models. Chapter 5 synthesizes insights from the review into strengthening the provision of youth job-matching services and provides recommendations for policies and practices to strengthen national ecosystems for youth job matching. A final chapter concludes.

9 A focus on migration is not in scope of this report. Models that aim to improve labor mobility through intra- or inter-country migration are not studied.

10 However, information on some programs was translated into English so it could be read by the authors.

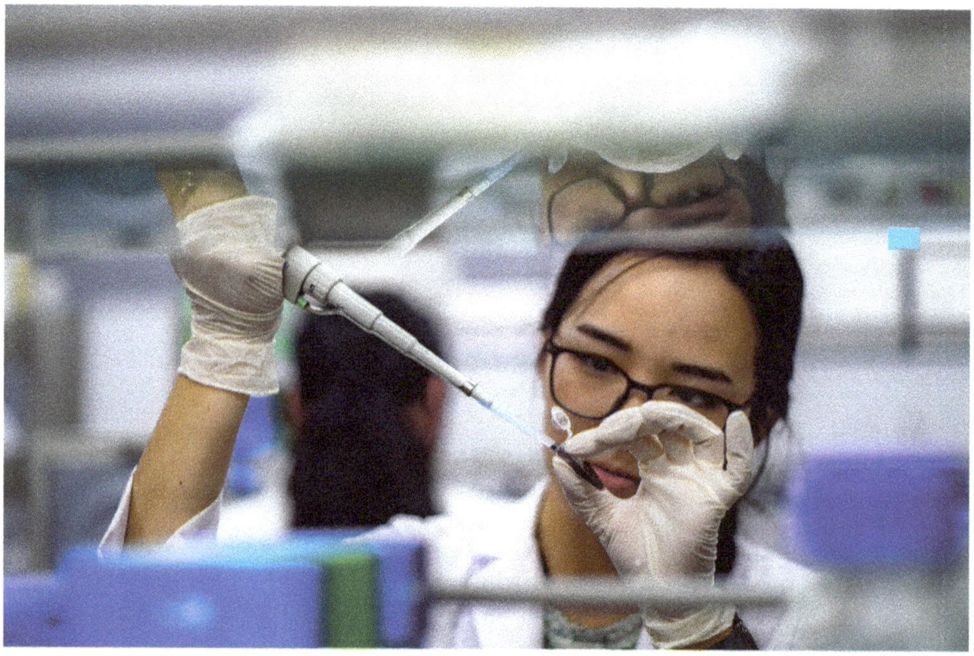

2

ROLE OF JOB MATCHING IN YOUTH EMPLOYMENT TRANSITIONS

This chapter summarizes job-matching theory and evidence for youth. It explains how job-matching support can benefit both young job seekers in strengthening their employment transitions as well as employers in reducing their recruitment costs. It examines trends of how young people find work and innovations in job-matching services, which will help situate the findings of the review. Uses of digital technologies in job matching are also highlighted.

2.1 What Is the Job-Matching Situation for Youth?

Job matching is central to the efficient functioning of labor markets and is particularly helpful for marginalized groups. Workers find jobs and employers fill vacancies through job matching. Job search and staff recruitment processes for both job seekers and employers are costly and time-consuming, however. Recruitment costs increase when employers struggle to find employable youth and effectively communicate their hiring needs, and search costs grow when young job seekers lack information about where and how to find jobs and to communicate their value. Efficient job matching reduces the costs of search and recruitment for both parties. For job seekers, the goal is to speed the transition to a quality job in line with their skills, interests, and aspirations, and, when unemployed, to minimize loss of earnings and human capital. For employers, the goal is to minimize the cost of securing good-fit (i.e., high-productivity) candidates (Figure 2).

Job matching is a dynamic process that involves transitions between various states of work and nonwork. These states can include wage or salaried employment, self-employment, unemployment, inactivity, and education and training. A young person may search for a new job while holding an existing job or may seek to transition between inactivity and work.

> Job matching is a dynamic process that involves transitions between various states of work and nonwork.

Figure 2: Matching Supply and Demand of Youth Labor

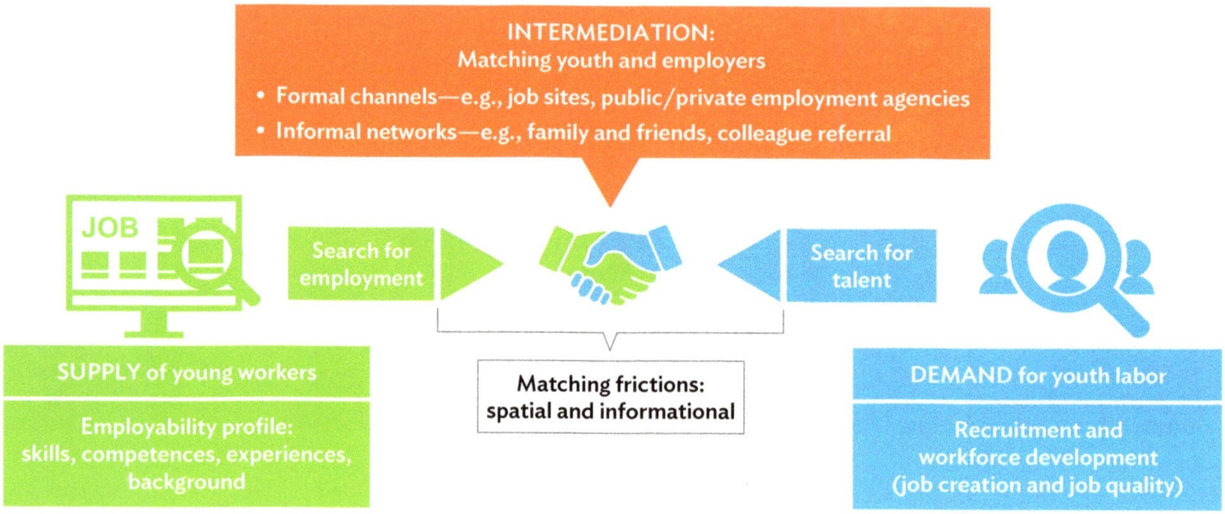

Source: Authors.

Job matching involves massive heterogeneities in the labor market. Each job seeker has a unique profile in terms of skills, attributes, credentials, and preferences and is searching among multiple jobs for a suitable position. There are a host of factors that determine a young person's choice to accept a job (Box 2). Job matching supports individual decisions and behaviors by both job seekers and employers. It also drives macro-level outcomes of employment, unemployment, and inactivity for the overall labor market. In other words, matching is a process between two parties that determines the wider situation of employment (Yashif 2007, Bassi and Nansamba 2017). Seminal work from the 1970s to 1990s provided a framework to consider the dynamics of how job seekers and employers make decisions about searching, hiring, and staying employed (i.e., the Diamond-Mortensen-Pissarides model) (Mortensen and Pissarides 1994, Diamond 1982).

The job-matching process is characterized by frictions, which can be particularly difficult for youth. Two main types of frictions are spatial mismatches and information asymmetries. Spatial mismatches exist between where job seekers reside and where vacancies are located (Wasmer and Zenou 2005). Indeed, location and mobility of young job seekers can affect their access to quality jobs. The ability to move for work is affected by factors that include transport infrastructure, cost of travel, and family permission. Information asymmetries exist when employers do not have good information about a young person's skills and attributes, and the job seeker does not have good information about where suitable jobs exist. Youth may also lack information on their own value (Carranza et al. 2021, J-PAL 2023). Lack of experience and qualifications can disadvantage youth when they compete for jobs against more mature workers, as youth have fewer references from past jobs (Groh et al. 2015). Young job seekers rely more on providing information about their skills and attributes to compensate for having less experience. Good information may be difficult to generate—especially in low-income contexts, because there, the labor market is often informal, as are job matching and other employment practices (Pritchett 2013).

Box 2

Why Young People Reject or Quit Jobs: Wage and Nonwage Preferences

Reservation wage. Youth will generally only accept job offers if the wage equals or exceeds their reservation wage (i.e., the minimum wage that workers are willing to accept). For some youth, their reservation wage is above what is realistic. This unreal expectation will be revised downward as job seekers learn more about realistic wages for their qualifications and desired jobs.

Utility reservation. A host of nonwage factors also determines employment choices and transitions. Key factors are benefits, flexible working arrangements, safety, and commuting time. These preferences are unique to each job seeker. These factors also tend to relate mostly to the formal labor market where nonwage benefits are more available. Benefits or safety may be less relevant to informal and low-income workers, because for them, work is a survival strategy—they often have no option but to accept the conditions outright. Researchers have assessed the relative influence of financial and nonfinancial considerations on deciding to accept jobs, but this has been primarily focused on developed countries. A study in the United States found that if nonwage factors are bundled and compared against wages, gains in nonwage utility are the chief cause of around one-third of job moves.

Prestige reservation. This is highly cultural and embedded in social norms about which types of jobs are held in high regard as well as intergenerational norms regarding parents' or caregivers' views of young people's employment decisions. This has been particularly studied in the Arab States and North Africa, where there are clear norms that place a high value on public sector jobs compared to private sector jobs, entrepreneurship, and low-skilled and low-paying jobs. There are also high levels of unemployment among educated youth in that region, which may be caused by considerations of prestige. Research in Jordan, for instance, showed that significant numbers of young job seekers provided with job-matching services turned down job interviews, rejected offers, or quickly quit jobs after placement. This was due to three types of nonwage preferences: prestige and the perceived social costs of working in a particular job, cultural appropriateness (especially among young women), and unwillingness to take jobs that were monotonous or required hard work. In surveys, 84% of job candidates identified the type of work as more important than the salary offered. Furthermore, among firms who agreed that Jordanian youth are less willing to take low-paid, less-skilled jobs than youth in other countries, almost half (48%) attributed this to concern about family prestige.

Sources: Sullivan and To (2011), Groh et al. (2015).

Young job seekers may not know their own value in the labor market. For some young people, failing to indicate the relevant skills that they possess (i.e., skills-signaling gap) may be a larger problem than their lack of industry skills (i.e., skills gap) (Barbarasa, Barret and Goldin 2017). On the other hand, for educated youth, formal qualifications may no longer be sufficient to signal their skills, as employers are increasingly looking for alternative assessment results and credentials, such as for digital skills (ADB and LinkedIn 2022, WEF 2020). Thus, young people can be inefficient in their job searches, because they may not know which jobs match their skills and profiles. As a result, they may end their searches early, becoming inactive or remaining in low-quality jobs (Belot, Kircher, and Muller 2019; Conlon et al. 2018). Job fairs not only allow young people to find work but also teach them about their value in the market, helping them adjust their expectations (Abebe et al. 2017, Beam 2016, Hayashi and Matsuda 2022).

Information and other frictions lead to poor decisions by employers. With limited information about job seekers' skills, firms may hire poorly matched workers and pay wages that are too high or too low for the workers' skills (Carranza et al. 2021). This reduces efficient labor allocation and ultimately affects business productivity. To make good matching decisions, employers need accurate information about candidates. In addition, for matches to last, employers must define the tasks and roles of new positions and properly market new vacancies.

Identifying and hiring talent is a major challenge for businesses. It can significantly impact business growth, especially for small and medium-sized enterprises (SMEs). Recruiting and managing talent[11] was noted to be the second-biggest challenge facing a global sample of 800 SMEs post-pandemic, behind survival and expansion (WEF and National University of Singapore 2022). It was considered more important than access to capital, culture and values, technology and innovation, and the policy environment (WEF and National University of Singapore 2022). Although a cost, hiring is a key activity for employers. More employers are offering on-the-job training and work placements such as internships and apprenticeships to upskill labor in line with their needs. Employers are looking for effective matching models that can help with recruitment.

2.2 How Do Youth Search for Work?

There has been a major uplift in digital job matching. Digital technologies are disrupting the work that young people do, skill sets that they need, as well as how they search for work and how job preparation services are delivered. This is the growing industry of JobTech, which includes digital platforms that connect people to work opportunities.[12] Digital job-matching platforms are creating new spaces for young job seekers and employers to connect and can strengthen such connectivity. Young people—especially those who are educated—are more likely than adults to use online job search and matching services (Okubo and Sakurai 2015;[13] Karaoglu, Hargittai, and Nguyen 2022). For example, in the United States, from 1998–2000 to 2008–2009, the share of unemployed youth (i.e., those ages 23–29 years) who used the internet to look for work tripled from 24% to 74% (Kuhn and Mansour 2011). In Mexico, the use of the internet and social media for job matching also increased among youth, while in-person employment services for this cohort flatlined between 2005 and 2019 (Chacaltana and Dasgupta 2021).

The use of digital job search and matching depends on age and other factors. These factors include internet access, digital job search know-how, digital platform awareness, education, and ethnicity. Digital services dominate recruitment methods used by employers, especially in developed markets.

11 Includes recruitment, retention, upskilling and training, and staff development.

12 Jobtech Alliance is a growing community of start-ups, funders, supporters, policymakers, and researchers defining and developing the JobTech ecosystem, focused on Africa. Other types of JobTech platforms include digital services for micro enterprises, tech-enabled skilling, and digital tools for worker enablement. JobTech draws on other emerging industries, such as FinTech (finance), EdTech (education), and AgTech (agriculture). See Jobtech Alliance.

13 Based on a survey in 2014 of more than 13,000 individuals from 13 countries, including Australia, the People's Republic of China, India, and Japan.

In the United States, 80%–90% of job postings requiring at least a bachelor's degree can be found online; the rate is lower for less skilled work, with 40%–60% of job postings requiring a high school diploma posted on the internet (Carnevale, Jayasundera, and Repnikov 2014). Digital services use also increased because of the COVID-19 pandemic. In Australia, for instance, the use of all types of digital recruitment channels by employers grew between 2020 and 2021 (Figure 3).

Figure 3: Recruitment Methods Used by Employers in Australia, 2020–2021
(%)

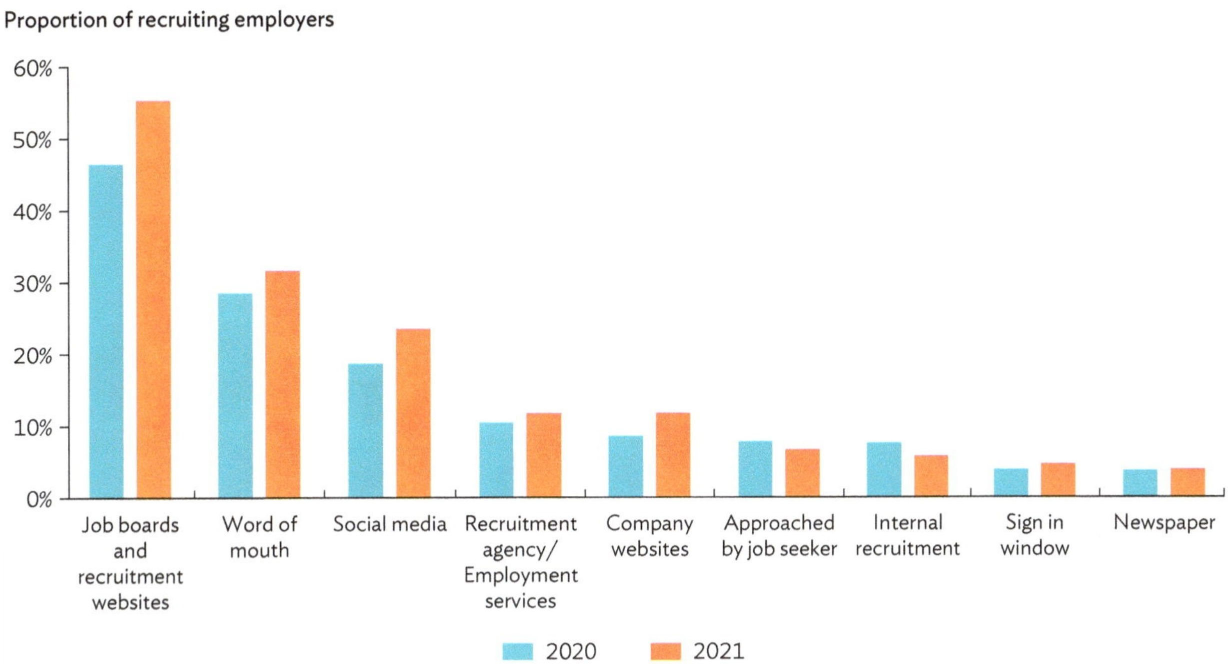

Source: Government of Australia. Recruitment Methods.

Employer use of digital channels varies by the type of job but does include entry-level jobs for youth. For example, in the European Union, employers' degree of use of online recruitment varies by size of firm (i.e., used more by large firms), sector (i.e., used less for construction, agriculture, and hospitality), skills level (i.e., used more for medium and highly skilled), and geography (i.e., used more for urban jobs) (Cedefop 2019). The global professional networking platform, LinkedIn, has a large share of entry-level job postings, although, on average, users are aged over 30 years (Box 3).

Innovations in digital job matching are expanding opportunities for youth. The volume and range of data on online job platforms have opened possibilities for smarter job matching and expanded real-time labor market information. Artificial intelligence (AI) and machine learning have transformed the matching process. The private sector has led many of these innovations with sophisticated screening algorithms that are driving faster, more accurate data-led matching that will continuously improve over time. Applications of these innovations are explored in the review of job-matching models presented in Chapter 4.

Box 3

Youth and LinkedIn

LinkedIn is a global networking platform used for job matching, especially among educated professionals. Analysis of postings in Brazil, India, Indonesia, and South Africa revealed that, on average, more than half of job postings were for entry-level positions. Rates ranged from 44% in India to 70% in Brazil. Most users were older than age 30 years. Less than 10% of 78 million LinkedIn profiles were categorized as youth. However, young people who joined the platform were more active than older users. Also, youth had more professional connections than adults across the four countries (i.e., 128–220 versus 76–90 connections).

Source: Barbarasa, Barrett, Goldin (2017).

Mobile job searches are also on the rise. In Malaysia, 65% of job seekers use mobile phones to search for jobs, and 21% use mobile phones to apply for jobs (HRAsia 2018). Other, more low-tech mobile services to reach informal workers are another important area of innovation. As the following chapter highlights, the number of mobile-based job-matching platforms for blue-collar workers has risen. Globally, over $80 million in investment was raised by leading digital blue-collar job platforms between 2014 and 2020 (Briter Bridges 2020).

Technology has the potential to "rewire" labor markets in line with real time and the future of work trends. Such digital approaches can redirect the labor supply toward demand, for example, by connecting job seekers with growth areas such as the digital or green economy. At the aggregate level, data analysis can map key trends in sector and occupational labor supply and demand as well as labor migration (McKinsey 2017). Shorter feedback loops are possible with more frequent generation of detailed data that can supplement traditional labor market information, particularly in countries and areas where official statistics are not regularly generated (ILO 2020a). This can also underpin stronger anticipatory capabilities of employment services to guide skills planning and support for job creation (Andersen, Feiler, and Schulz 2016).

Youth-targeted job matching services are a focus of digital innovation at public employment services. Labor market support is a major area of service digitalization among governments. The COVID-19 pandemic spurred a digital leap in this regard. The share of public employment services (PES) in Organisation for Economic Co-operation and Development (OECD) members that offer digital services delivery increased from around 50% pre-pandemic to around 80% post-pandemic. Today, more than two in five countries are engaging in developments using AI or other advanced tools to support job matching. The use of advanced technologies among PES, however, is lower for the delivery of complex services, such as counseling, case management, and self-assessment (OECD 2022c). The job-matching service is the primary user of advanced technologies by PES globally and is jointly first, with labor market information, in low- and middle-income countries.[14]

[14] Other uses include registration, counseling and case management, and access to skills training.

Figure 4: Use of Technologies in Public Employment Services by Target Group
(%)

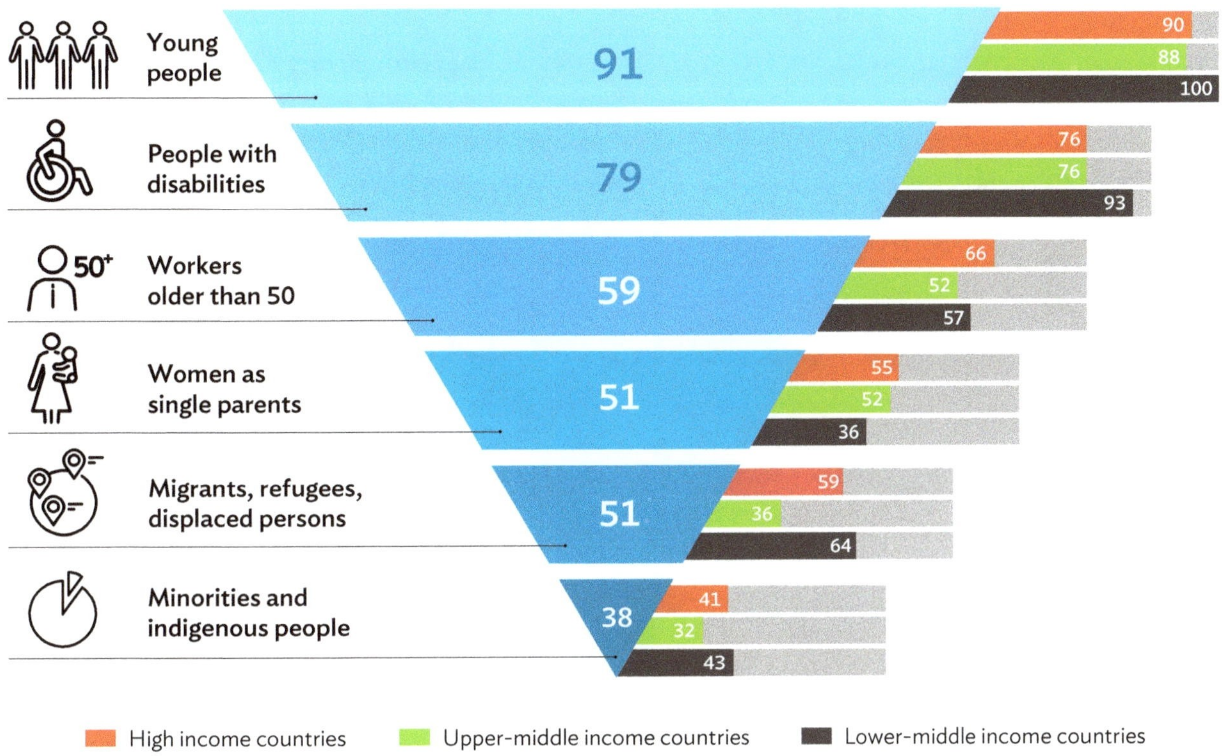

Notes: Figure shows percentage of public employee service users who responded to a 2020 International Labour Organization survey on technology usage. Sixty-nine valid responses to the survey were generated.

Source: ILO (2022b).

Youth are the main target group for these technology-facilitated services compared to other disadvantaged groups (ILO 2022b) (Figure 4).

However, youth engagement with public employment services is low, as young people often rely on informal networks to find jobs. On average between 2019 and 2021 across 29 OECD members, the share of unemployed youth (i.e., those ages 15–29 years) who contacted PES or used their vacancy announcements was only 40%. This means that most were conducting their job searches via other channels. Some governments increased funding in 2022 to strengthen job outreach to unregistered NEET youth, including Australia and the Republic of Korea (OECD 2022c).

In Uzbekistan, youth are more likely to use private than public digital job-matching services. In a self-reinforcing cycle, many employers do not post their vacancies with PES. Thus, young job seekers who do register with PES only find less relevant, low-skilled, low-paid postings (Honorati and Marguerie 2021). In Indonesia, only one in five young people find jobs using digital technologies, with the majority relying on personal connections (Figure 5). Indeed, among unemployed youth, the most popular search channels remain family and social networks. This is the case for over 40% of youth in the Philippines (Figure 5).

Figure 5: Job Search Channels among Young Job Seekers in Indonesia and the Philippines

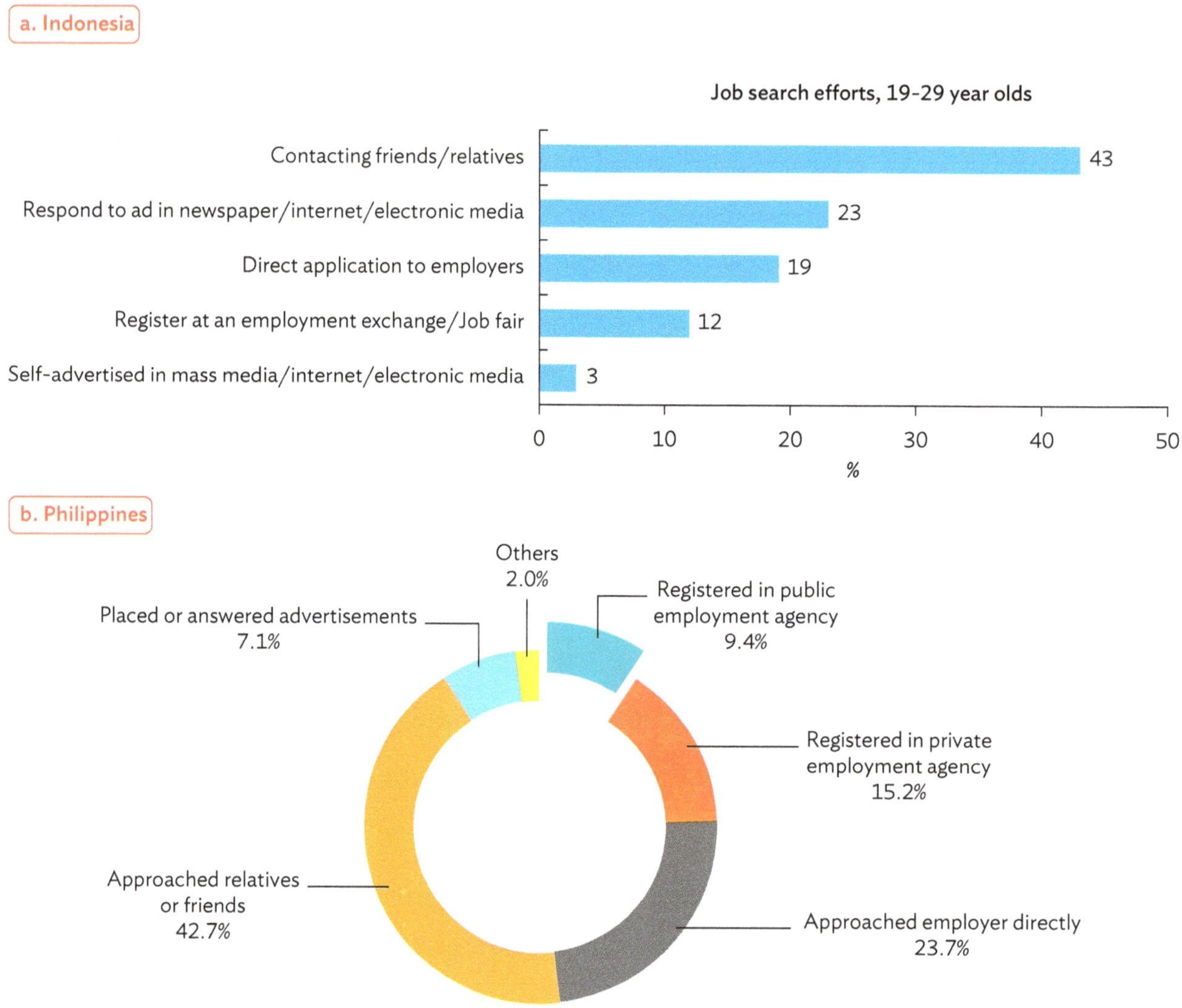

Sources: BPS (2019) and Philippines Statistics Authority (2022).

The choice of a job search channel is determined by multiple factors and can entrench disadvantage. Thus, young people's capacity to search effectively for work varies. Being able to navigate the labor market is itself a skill and requires knowledge; emotional capital (i.e., self-esteem and motivation); and social capital (i.e., networks and role models). Foundational factors[15] intersect with young people's employability profiles and ultimately determine their confidence and readiness to search and to apply for work. For youth experiencing cumulative barriers to labor market inclusion—

[15] These are fundamental socioeconomic characteristics that shape a young person's job potential, including family background (i.e., the education and employment experiences of parents/caregivers); community background (i.e., prevailing aspiration levels and presence of role models); and personal attributes (i.e., confidence, self-esteem, and ambition) (Bird and Silva 2020).

including those with disabilities, early school leavers, and migrants—relatives and friends are particularly important channels for job searches. However, such marginalized youth tend to have narrower social networks, which can restrict their access to job information and openings. They are also more likely to be connected with other people of a similar (i.e., disadvantaged) background and social identity. As a result, the people in their networks are less likely to have or to know of quality jobs or to be able to connect them to quality job opportunities. Their networks are also less likely to include role models that can motivate them to look for quality work (Chacaltana and Dasgupta 2021).

2.3 What Works in Youth Job Matching?

Job matching is among the most promising approaches to address the youth employment challenge. Indeed, the literature shows that effective job-matching interventions lead to better employment and earnings outcomes (Apunyo et al. 2022, Generation Unlimited 2018, ILO 2020a, Sing and Liu 2020, J-PAL 2018). In addition, there is growing recognition of the need to integrate job matching into training programs to improve employment outcomes. A key research finding is the positive effect of work-based learning and work experience as a part of education, for example, through mentors, internships, and apprenticeships (Hovhannisyan et al. 2022). Training does not necessarily lead to employment—this depends on the nature and quality of the training as well as the availability of quality job openings (Kluve et al. 2017, ILO 2022c). A recent synthesis of evidence identified job placement as an important dimension to ensure that vocational training graduates find employment (J-PAL 2023). A study in India concluded that the variation in employment outcomes of training programs highlights the necessity of a "proper policy toward engaging trained individuals to avoid the massive loss of human capital and the resources invested in training them" (Mitra 2022). A study in Sri Lanka similarly recommended that a proper mechanism be developed to improve links with industries to boost employment opportunities for trainees (Padmakanthi 2022).

> There is growing recognition of the need to integrate job matching into training programs to improve employment outcomes.

Reducing information asymmetries between job seekers and employers benefits both parties. This is especially relevant for youth without certified education or training. Skills assessment certificates can be helpful in demonstrating competencies, especially when developed according to industry preferences and a national qualifications framework. Letters of reference or recommendations can also convey valuable information about job seekers' skill sets, including soft skills. For example, some participants in a New York City summer jobs program were given recommendation letters by their supervisors, which were used by the participants to seek subsequent work. The randomized cohort who received letters were more likely to be employed the following year by 3 percentage points, and their earnings 4 years later were $1,349 higher than the cohort that did not receive letters (Heller and Kessler 2022).

A study in Uganda tested the effects of giving information about hard-to-observe soft skills of workers to employers and job seekers at the recruitment stage.[16] At job interviews, certificates documenting the results of these assessments were given to both hiring managers and job candidates in five skills domains—attendance, communication skills, creativity, trustworthiness, and willingness to help others. As a result of this information, hiring managers revised their views of the candidates' skills upward, especially those of managers. Young interviewees who saw that they had good soft skills updated their employment aims, by, for example, raising their reservation wage or deciding to return to training with the intent to transition into better jobs. Yet, this only happened if they were matched to managers who revised their beliefs first—young people reacted only if the employers reacted positively (Bassi and Nansamba 2017).

Having better soft skills increased the candidates' probabilities of being hired, with young job seekers in the middle of the soft skills distribution most likely to be offered jobs. Candidates with low levels of soft skills confirmed the preexisting beliefs of the potential employers, while those with the highest levels were less likely to be offered jobs. Interestingly, they were considered less likely to accept offers or more likely to leave due to their new beliefs about finding better jobs elsewhere. This study showed how giving both parties the same information can affect job matching, which is known as "two-sided symmetric learning" (Bassi and Nansamba 2017).

Tailoring support to a young person's individual profile is key to successful job matching. Different matching models cater to different youth cohorts, for example, by skills level. The quantity, range, intensity, and sequencing of services can vary. More intensive support offerings can fill employability gaps and address complex nonemployment[17] barriers. Young persons ready to enter the job market can be supported by getting them interviews with employers aligned to their skill set and aspirations. On the other hand, young people who are not quire ready requires a wider range of services tailored to their needs. These may include psychosocial counseling, workplace etiquette training, obtaining funds for transport or proper clothing, and skills training. For example, youth support services, including PES, can be classified at three levels based on youth job readiness: (i) mainstream support, which comprises improving job search skills for job-ready youth; (ii) assisted services, such as addressing employability deficits; and (iii) intensive support, including addressing complex nonemployment barriers. Profiling and classification have emerged as key activities for youth employment providers. Assessing young people, creating employment profiles (including psychosocial attributes), and steering them to appropriate support services require advanced capabilities in case management (Chacaltana and Dasgupta 2021, Loxha and Morgandi 2014).

Job-matching success should be measured over a long time frame. Matching success should not only be measured by whether matches are made. The quality of the matches is crucial, which is often reflected in how long people stay in matched positions. If a young person is placed into a job but then soon leaves and becomes inactive, the match was not successful.

[16] The informal labor market setting makes the results particularly useful and involved vocational education graduates and SMEs.

[17] It is argued in the next chapter that this binary distinction between employment and non-employment barriers is becoming less relevant to describing the complexities of a young person's employment profile.

Job matching thus has quality and sustainability dimensions. Young people benefit most from staying in jobs long enough to improve their earnings and to accumulate the skills and experience necessary to enable an onward transition to a higher-quality job. For employers, longer matches mean reaping productivity gains that more than cover the costs of recruitment and onboarding.

> **Matching success should not only be measured by whether matches are made. The quality of the matches is crucial.**

Tackling only a single constraint can render job-matching effectiveness short-lived. For example, providing a transport subsidy means youth can access locations with better jobs (or with better information about job vacancies). However, if they are not given further support to make good job matches or to retain their jobs, the benefits of the subsidy will fade over time. Similarly, cash transfers can help marginalized youth afford job searches, and vouchers can be provided to attend job fairs, but complementary assistance may be needed to gain the benefits of long-term positions (J-PAL 2023). Job-matching services that support fluid, progressive employment transitions of youth—ultimately resulting in quality jobs—are key.

Job matching can also help create a more equitable labor market. Targeted support for disadvantaged groups can enhance their access to quality jobs. For example, young people with disabilities face additional constraints in entering the labor market, but making positive early transitions can set up healthy and productive life courses. While training and job preparation are valuable, directly connecting such youth with employers and work placements (to gain experience) can tackle barriers such as discrimination and negative hiring practices.[18] In addition, models that reach and support marginalized youth can also help employers tap into a more diverse pool of skilled labor.

Gaps in evidence remain on how to structure successful youth job-matching services. In particular, there is limited evidence on developing economies and informal employment environments. Moreover, evaluations that have been conducted often do not measure longer-term impacts. For example, if people are placed into jobs with fixed-term contracts, the gain in employment cannot be sustained (Cottier et al. 2018). Evidence is also lacking on the substitution and displacement effects of job matching (J-PAL 2018). Interventions create net benefits only when workers matched via targeted programs do not crowd out nontargeted workers.

Finally, little is known about how best to meet the needs of employers through job-matching interventions. Research has shown the importance of generating information about candidate skills and competencies to make good matches, as noted above. However, the role of matching in broader human resources processes is understudied. These processes include job profiling, onboarding, human resources strategies, and workforce development. Job matching can be one part of a larger support package that employers use to recruit and to retain workers. Figure 6 illustrates the fit of the job-matching function in the broader human resources planning processes of recruitment (including preparation and search), retention, and staff development.

18 Several specialist matching models were identified in the region and are discussed in Chapter 4.

Figure 6: Job Matching and Complementary Services for Employers and Job Seekers

HR = human resources.

Source: Authors.

Evidence gaps also relate to technology-based job matching. What works best to leverage digital technology to optimize job matching for youth is not well understood, including the kind of information that results in the best job matches and how it can be best exchanged. Also unclear are how low-tech approaches can best include marginalized youth as well as the right blend of public and private services in delivery. The full potential of technology has not yet been reached; matching inefficiencies still characterize labor markets, including high rates of labor underutilization, turnover, and offer rejections (Groh et al. 2015). As one researcher noted, "It remains an open question about how best to design online markets that match workers to firms" (Pople 2020). The pace of innovation and scarcity of evidence mean that it is important to take stock of current practices. Learning from proven and promising approaches can help generate a knowledge base to guide policymakers and other stakeholders in strengthening job matching for youth as part of addressing the youth employment challenge in Asia and the Pacific.

> It remains an open question about how best to design online markets that match workers to firms.
>
> — Pople (2020)

3

A FRAMEWORK FOR YOUTH EMPLOYMENT TRANSITIONS

This chapter assesses the labor market situation of youth in terms of employment transitions. Understanding the complexities that young people face in their journeys to quality jobs is necessary to consider how job matching can be best designed and delivered. A conceptual framework on youth employment transitions will help advance thinking for policy and programs as well as guide assessment of key features and practices of youth job-matching approaches in the region.

3.1 What Are Youth Employment Transitions?

Understanding the nature of young people's employment transitions is critical to effective job matching. The previous chapter showed how the process of matching job seekers and employers emphasizes the transitions that people make into, back into, and within the job market. The nature of these transitions is different for youth. Young people are most likely to be in more than one labor market state (i.e., in work, out of work, and in education or training) at a time. For example, they may be managing a "side hustle" selling goods while completing a part-time training course and working in a fixed-term contract or regular job. Youth are also often making their first transitions from school into work (Schmid 2017; Vaccaro et al. 2022; Causa, Luu, and Abendschein 2021). A longitudinal study in Australia identified a type of labor market status specific only to youth (i.e., ages 15–24 years)—"churning with work"—which captures the youth-specific experience of moving in and out of employment. From young adults (i.e., ages 25–39 years) to mature adults (i.e., ages 40–54 years) and seniors (i.e., ages 55–64 years), work became more of a steady state (Box 4).

At the macro level, the (re)allocation of labor is central to enhancing productivity and inclusivity. The labor market needs to evolve continually in step with the dynamics of how jobs are created, sought, and filled. Transitions are a particularly useful concept for unpacking the employment experience of youth. Youth is a time of major shifts in a young person's development—from learning to earning and from dependency to independence. The distinct nature of youth transitions thus guides how job matching can best serve their needs.

> Youth is a time of major shifts in a young person's development—from learning to earning and from dependency to independence.

Box 4

Employment Transitions of a Youth Cohort in Australia, 2000–2010

A 2013 study in Australia identified five labor market pathways specific to young people (i.e., ages 15–24 years). Although covering 2000–2010, this analysis over a 10-year period provides valuable insights into the nature of employment transitions for youth. The five pathways involved distinct types of experiences and transitions compared to those for older workers. The five pathways were defined as education to work, work and study to work, churning with work, work with or without study, and a prolonged not-in-labor-force phase.

Youth (i.e., ages 15–24 years) were the only age cohort that included "churning with work" as an activity type. From young adults (i.e., ages 25–39 years) to mature adults (i.e., ages 40–54 years) and seniors (i.e., ages 55–64 years), work was a steady state. However, over half of youth churned—moved into and out of work—over the 10-year study period.

The figure below shows how much time individuals of different ages spent on different activities. For youth, "churning with work" was the main activity. For the majority, work was interspersed with other activities, such as unemployment or study. On average, youth on the "churning with work" pathway undertook about three out of five activities. They each had at least one work spell (and an average of 2.9 spells), lasting an average of 32 months. About 71% had an average of two spells (an average of 9.4 months) of work and study combined. Spells of work could include job changes. The gender divide was even.

For the cohort of young adults at the beginning of the 10-year period, 63% were on the work pathway. They had greater continuity in employment relative to the youth cohort. About one-third were on the work pathway throughout the 10 years. The average number of spells in work was two, lasting 54 months (i.e., 4.5 years) per spell.

continued on next page

Box 4 *continued*

Average Labor Market Time Allocations of People in Australia, 2000–2010

NILF = not in the labor force.

Notes:

1. The time allocation for each activity represents the total percentage of the 10-year period spent undertaking that activity, averaged over individuals in that age segment and pathway.
2. The average time that individuals spent on an activity is not necessarily one continuous stretch, and the ordering of activities shown is not related to the underlying patterns in the sequences.
3. The study analyzed data from the Household, Income and Labour Dynamics in Australia (HILDA) Survey. Labor market activities of a sample of 6,566 individuals were tracked each month from July 2000 to June 2010, based on a categorization of education and work activities.

Source: Fry and Boulton (2013).

Employment transitions for youth are often nonlinear. The pathways young people take from school into work and through their initial employment experiences usually do not occur in a linear progression. Due to the barriers that young people face in obtaining quality jobs, they typically zigzag through the job market (Iskander and Rankin 2019). When young people begin to navigate the world of work, they undertake multiple transitions, which are fluid and often fragile. Their labor market pathways crisscross earning and learning, activity and inactivity, and aspiration and discouragement. The first transition into work is a process, not a one-off. Youth may lose their first jobs and need to bounce back.[19] For low-income youth, multiple gigs may be necessary to "get by" (Barford and Coombe 2019). Educated youth may balance self-education and lifelong learning with work to improve prospects and to respond to changing employer demands (OECD 2022b).

A fixed destination of full-time formal employment is not the reality for most youth, especially in developing countries. Thinking purely this way can be problematic (Andersen, Feiler, and Schulz 2016). Young people today make more frequent job and occupation changes than previous generations and engage more in nonstandard contracts than adults (ILO 2021b). Youth employment transitions involve multiple pathways that are not sequenced. Some have suggested that the concept of transitions creates false binaries, for example, between education and work, or youth and adults. Alternatives aim to be more in line with the nonlinear reality of youth, such as "critical moments" or "vital conjectures" (Jones 2022). In this report, the concept of transitions is considered instructive and valuable when understood in terms of the complexity, multiplicity, and nonlinear nature of young people's trajectories into, back into, and within the labor market.

Young people's first transitions from school into work are foundational to future trajectories and outcomes. If young people do not make good first transitions into employment, the disadvantages that they experience compound over time in terms of job quality, earnings, and mental health, known as "scarring effects" (O'Higgins 1997). There is growing evidence that early transitions are predictive of longer-term labor market experiences and outcomes (Cebulla and Whetton 2018). For more than 7 in 10 people ages 15–24 years, the first contact with the labor market is through informal employment (Chacaltana and Dasgupta 2021). When young people's first experiences are long-term unemployment, they are likely to move between stages of unemployment and low-wage employment throughout their entire working lives.

Studies to measure the time that young people take to transition from school to stable work have found long transition intervals. In Mongolia, it takes, on average, 7 years for young people to find stable and satisfactory work; it takes tertiary graduates 4 years (Matsumoto and Elder 2010). Long transitions from school to work can have negative repercussions for morale and lifelong productivity.

Young people make employment transitions alongside other life transitions that together define their stage of life. People experience marital, family, and reproductive changes as well as formative citizenship during their youth (Chacaltana, Elder, and Lee 2019; World Bank 2006).

[19] Note that this has important implications for the measurement time frames of employment outcomes. For example, one study of unemployment in the United States looked at durable jobs and assessed successful matching 2, 3, and up to 15 months from taking up a new post (Hall and Schulhofer-Wohl 2015).

Decisions young people take shape their future life trajectories (ILO 2019a). Importantly, youth is both a stage of life and a stage in the life cycle. This dual dynamic of being young—shaped by the experience of youth itself—and transitioning from childhood to adulthood is key to comprehending the complexity of the youth experience. It "calls for a more dynamic understanding of youth transitions among policymakers and those designing youth employment programmes" (Sanderson 2019). Youth should be viewed "as both a stage of 'being' and 'becoming,' ... both a condition in its own right but also part of the life course process" (Sanderson 2019). This has important implications for designing labor market policies for youth and more broadly for shaping human capital systems that are responsive to life-cycle needs (Bird and Silva 2020, Schady et al. 2023).

> **This is a crucial period of life when young women and men have to make important decisions that will lay the foundations for lifelong professional and personal development.**
>
> **— ILO (2019a)**

3.2 What Constrains Youth Employment Transitions?

Young people face multiple, interconnected constraints when making employment transitions. As well as barriers associated with inefficient job matching, the constraints young people face are shaped by factors affecting the supply of and demand for youth labor, plus the capacity of the youth employment support system. These factors are discussed in this section. Supply issues cover quantity and quality of the young workforce—the quantity of youth labor supply varies according to demographic trends and the desire of young people to enter the labor market, and the quality of supply is affected by education level as well as by foundational factors that determine a young person's capability to navigate transitions. The demand for youth labor determines how many jobs are available to youth from employers and through entrepreneurship. It is affected by a range of socioeconomic megatrends, including climate change, technological progress, and demographics. In addition, the quality and coverage of youth employment support services also impact youth's access to work opportunities and their potential to thrive at work.

On the supply side, many young people lack skills and the readiness to work. They are under-skilled, or their skills are not matched to the vacancies available—they are overqualified or underqualified (i.e., a vertical mismatch) or do not possess the necessary skills (i.e., a horizontal mismatch). Across youth of all education levels, there is generally a lack of adequate transferable skills, including foundational, cognitive, and socio-emotional.[20] For example, South Asia lags globally in preparing youth for the world of work. It is estimated that 54% of youth there will leave school in the next decade unequipped with the basic skills to obtain quality jobs.[21]

[20] See Lyon, Ranzani, Rosati (2020); OECD (2015); and World Bank. Skills Development.

[21] The 2019 data are from the 2030 Skills Scorecard, which combines (projected) secondary school completion rates and attainment of basic workplace skills. See UNICEF (2019a) and Global Business Coalition for Education (2019).

The youth labor supply is also affected by foundational factors that shape capacities and vulnerabilities. Young people's accumulating life experiences define their youth and shape their labor market outcomes. These experiences are a combination of internal and external factors. Internal factors are personal attributes such as self-confidence, whereas external factors relate to political and economic forces and social norms. Together, they shape young people's capability for gaining employment. Negative external factors, such as social exclusion, reduce the chances of a successful life course.[22] Social environments determine not only the materiality of what is possible for youth but also their perceptions and aspirations (Huijsmans, Ansell, and Froerer 2021). Aspirations can play a pivotal role in shaping young people's employment transitions.[23] A recent evidence gap map looked at welfare[24] outcomes of youth as well as skills, employment, and earnings. Impact evaluations found that a major flaw of youth employment interventions is failing to account for these other factors that can influence outcomes (Apunyo et al. 2022).

Regional demographics have put further pressure on employment prospects for youth. Globally, Asia and the Pacific has the highest projected rise in the median age of the labor force (ILO 2018b). The share of the population ages 65 years and older in the region is projected to increase from 10% in 2022 to 30% in 2100 (UNESCAP 2022). The pace of aging varies across the region, which shapes the investment window to maximize the demographic dividend. For example, in some economies, the number of young people ages 15–29 years will continue to increase up to 2050, including in Kazakhstan, Mongolia, Pakistan, and most Pacific developing member countries.[25] As populations age, the available workforce shrinks, which creates demand for younger workers. Yet, those who are working need to be more productive to compensate for a higher dependency ratio. In countries and areas with higher numbers of working-age people, youth face greater competition from experienced workers.

On the demand side, quality jobs are scarce to absorb young labor market entrants. The availability of jobs for youth is a function of the overall demand for labor in an economy. If jobs are scarce overall, youth will be affected. In a recession, younger workers are typically the first to be laid off, in part because they are easier to make redundant due to lower levels of employment protection, but also because they have less experience (O'Higgins, Verick, and Elsheikhi 2021; ADB and ILO 2020). Even in periods of strong output growth, such growth is not always jobs-rich or inclusive of youth (World Bank 2012). For example, countries in South Asia have recorded strong growth but are not creating enough quality jobs to keep pace with a rising youth population. Between 2018 and 2025, over 1.8 million young people have or will reach working age every month in the subregion. To create enough jobs, double-digit growth rates are needed, assuming that the same job creation rates are maintained as those during 2005–2015. Meanwhile, the quality of jobs is a persistent challenge, as the levels of formal wage employment are low with widespread decent work deficits (World Bank 2017).

---

22 Social issues of exclusion or spatial issues that determine marginalization are sometimes considered nonemployment barriers. Arguably, this distinction is becoming less useful, as the complexity of the youth labor market experience is becoming better understood (ILO 2021c).

23 See, for example, Gardiner and Goedhuys (2020).

24 Welfare includes citizenship, family health, household income, inclusion and empowerment, and antisocial behavior.

25 Except New Zealand. Population percentages by age group are available for ages 15–24 years, not ages 15–29 years. This group will decline in the Pacific subregion (including Australia, designated by the United Nations as Oceania) from 2020 to 2050 by 1 percentage point. Data are from UNDESA (2019).

Across the entire region, a large share of young people are engaged in informal and nonstandard forms of work with low job quality (ILO 2016, ILO 2022a). Globally, adult workers (i.e., those ages 25 years or over) have higher job quality than young workers (Hovhannisyan et al. 2022).

Megatrends affecting the labor market also shape demand for young workers. The opportunities available to young people and the trajectories that they take from school to work are increasingly determined by structural transformations and disruptions. These include globalization and value-chain integration, climate change, technological progress, and demographic change (ADB 2022c). These trends affect the jobs available to youth and the skills that they need now and in the future. Automation and digitalization are having a profound effect on industries, occupations, and skills demand. As technologies advance, job mismatches are inevitable. The lag between market signals for new skills and education system reform also deepens the mismatch (Palmer 2018). This structural problem is compounded by perceptions—if employers do not believe that youth have the right skills for new jobs, they will be less inclined to create those jobs. The share of employers who reported challenges in finding skilled workers increased in the region from 28% in 2006 to 48% in 2015 (Lee 2016).

Support systems to address the diverse and complex needs of youth are often fragmented. This fragmentation is another constraint facing youth in making positive employment transitions. Youth employment programs often do not account for the complex lived experiences of young people. In particular, they do not account for "the broad array of trajectories that people follow in the period that defines their youth" (Chacaltana, Elder, and Lee 2019). Diagnostic work for youth employment policymaking and programming is often insufficiently multidimensional. Also, informal employment has been overlooked as a focus of support (Andersen, Feiler, and Schulz 2016). This may grow as a problem, as flexible and nonstandard forms of work become more common among youth.

> Youth employment programs often do not account for the complex lived experiences of young people. In particular, they do not account for "the broad array of trajectories that people follow in the period that defines their youth."
>
> — Chacaltana, Elder, and Lee (2019)

The fragmentation is also evident at the institutional level. Even if policy frameworks are intended to connect different policy dimensions—such as housing, employment, and health—implementation capacity can be weak.[26] A disconnected support system can be confusing for youth to navigate, making it more likely that they give up. To address these challenges, there is a trend toward the aggregation or rationalization of youth-targeted public services, for example, through one-stop shops[27] that provide a single entry point to ease services access for youth. The most effective youth employment approaches integrate multiple types of support, tailored to the specific constraints faced by young people (Box 5).

[26] See also Youth Policy Labs. Global Youth Policy Reviews.

[27] One-stop shops have grown as a policy approach to rationalize services provision to citizens (OECD 2022a).

Box 5

What Works to Support Youth Employment?

The most effective youth employment approaches integrate multiple types of support, tailored to the specific constraints faced by young people. Integrated approaches combine supply-side, demand-side, and intermediation measures. They are highly personalized to the individual needs of young people depending on where they are in their employment transition. For example, secondary school students primarily need labor market preparation and orientation, such as career counseling. Youth not in employment, education, or training—often off the radar of public services—may need to be reached through peer-to-peer mechanisms and to undertake basic literacy and life skills training before they are ready to consider employment options. Integrated approaches also engage youth in program design and implementation across the program cycle, including in feedback loops for continuous improvement. Coordination across multiple stakeholders is required to design and to deliver these relevant, holistic solutions.

More is being learned about the different aspects of various support types that drive results. For example, on the demand side, directing young entrepreneurs away from saturated sectors and toward growth industries is more likely to lead to net benefits in a local economy. On the supply side, providing youth with workplace values and exposure (e.g., through internships or apprenticeships) can improve outcomes.

Analysis of a Government of Australia longitudinal survey of youth, which tracked young Australians over 10 years from their mid-teens to mid-twenties, found that providing enterprise skills (i.e., work-oriented soft skills like problem solving, communication, and teamwork) and paid work experience were the two most significant factors in accelerating a disadvantaged young person's transition into work. Obtaining employment in a future-focused sector and having an optimistic mindset were the next two most significant factors.

Providing these inputs could accelerate a young person's transition into work by 17 months. The average transition time from full-time education to full-time work for youth in the sample was 2.6 years. For students, the more time spent in paid work experience, the faster the school-to-work transition. For example, 2,000 hours of paid work (e.g., 10 hours per week, part-time, for 4 years) sped up the transition by 5 months compared to students without relevant experience; 5,000 hours of paid work (e.g., 25 hours per week, part-time, for 3 years and 2 months plus 2 lots of 3-month internships, working at least 35 hours per week) sped it up by 12 months.

Importantly, these inputs can help overcome socioeconomic disadvantages. Young people from deprived areas can catch up with peers from high socioeconomic areas if they receive enterprise skills and paid work experience, and their more advantaged peers do not. These inputs can even mean that youth from low socioeconomic areas can enter the full-time workforce faster than young people from high socioeconomic areas.

Sources: Foundation for Young Australians (2018); ADB (2022b).

The COVID-19 pandemic prompted some uplift in youth-targeted policymaking. This was the case at least in OECD members; in some cases, strengthened integration and ministerial coordination occurred at different levels of government. For example, Finland enhanced the capacity of service hubs, known as "cockpits," for youth under age 30 years to access a wide range of public services, such as education and employment, mental health, housing, and others (OECD 2022a).

Nevertheless, the lack of awareness of available support, lack of trust in public services, or poor services experiences can continue to constrain uptake (Chacaltana and Dasgupta 2021). A study of youth employment in Uzbekistan found that the public online job portal is "largely unknown to youth" and that those who did use it found the experience to be not user-friendly due to, for example, difficulties in registering (Honorati and Marguerie 2021).

3.3 How Can Policymakers Conceptualize and Support Youth Employment Transitions?

Policymaking for youth employment is evolving. The fluid nature of youth employment transitions—intersected with major shifts in health and well-being, family formation and independence, and civic life—means that the needs of young people relate to multiple dimensions of policy. These span financial inclusion, housing, transport, public health, and rural and urban development. Young people with poor mental health struggle to find the motivation to search for work or to hold down jobs. Others without access to good public transport are limited in their labor market outlook and opportunities. If young people have low levels of financial literacy or trust in financial institutions, they cannot maximize the benefits of earning.

The support young people need for employment transitions spans a spectrum from risk prevention to opportunity creation. At one end is disadvantaged young people who face complex and entrenched barriers to accessing quality jobs; at the other are educated and motivated youth who need to make optimal choices to maximize their labor market fit. This spectrum frames the range of support that governments and other stakeholders can provide, from tackling poverty and risk through social assistance to increasing capability and opportunity through career growth. It emphasizes connecting social protection and employment policy as well as integrating related policy domains. Further, applying a life-cycle lens to policymaking helps ensure that risks and potential gaps for youth are addressed (Bird and Silva 2020). Ensuring a coherent policy approach to youth employment is included in the SDGs; Indicator 8.b.1 calls for a "developed and operationalized national strategy for youth employment, as a distinct strategy or as part of a national employment strategy."[28]

A multidimensional conceptual framework for youth employment transitions can guide regional policy stakeholders in designing and implementing relevant youth employment support. The framework, developed by the authors, synthesizes the latest youth employment evidence in a structure that can support program planning and policy dialogue (Figure 7). This holistic picture of the youth experience of entering and navigating the labor market illustrates what is known about the determinants of youth employment outcomes. It includes the foundational factors that shape young people's needs in the labor market—the complexity, multiplicity, and nonlinear nature of their employment transitions into, back into, and within the labor market; integrated program packages that best tackle complex constraints; and the support architecture that can improve access to and connect policy domains.

[28] UN. Goal 8. Sustainable Development.

Figure 7: Youth Employment Transitions Framework

Source: Authors.

3.4 How Much Is Spent on Youth Employment Transitions in the Region?

The multifaceted nature of support systems that underpin youth employment transitions makes it difficult to define youth employment budgetary allocations. A full analysis of youth employment-related spending by a government requires data from multiple government departments and agencies at the national, regional, and local administrative levels. Based on the SDG indicators, the International Labour Organization (ILO) developed an online repository for national employment policies and youth employment strategies that aims to connect different policy domains and to advance comprehensive approaches.[29] It helps indicate policies for youth employment, but it does not provide information on expenditures.

Youth employment support combines general measures that support all age cohorts and youth-specific programs. The optimum policy package for youth employment combines the intentional inclusion of youth in macroeconomic and labor market policies with interventions targeted at improving their economic inclusion, especially that of disadvantaged youth. This combination helps ensure that youth are not left behind as economies grow. Youth also need special consideration during times of economic downturn and recovery. ADB and ILO (2020) noted that "[t]o support young people specifically during periods of constrained fiscal resources, such as the COVID-19 pandemic, governments need to balance (i) the inclusion of youth in wider labour market and economic recovery measures with (ii) youth-targeted interventions to maximize efficiency in the allocation of resources." This adds further complexity to disentangling youth employment-related expenditure.

Regarding social protection, youth access is limited and fragmented, which further complicates analysis of expenditures. Social protection can play an important role in protecting out-of-work youth and reactivating labor market inclusion. Yet, from young people's perspectives, access and eligibility can be restricted. First-time workers are usually not eligible for contributory schemes due to lack of tenure. For noncontributory support, youth are typically not the primary target and can fall through the cracks. They are often too old to receive child benefits, and, if they still live with their parents or other caregivers, they cannot access head-of-household schemes even if they play significant earning roles in the household (UNDESA 2018, Bird and Silva 2020, Mueller et al. 2022).

Overall, expenditure on labor market programs is low in the region, compared with other types of social protection. ADB has pioneered work since 2005 to monitor spending on social protection at the country and regional levels. Its analysis shows that budgetary allocations toward labor market programs overall are low compared to allocations for other types of social protection. The average allocation for labor market programs in Asia and the Pacific is 0.1% of GDP, compared with 1.1% of GDP allocated to social assistance. In addition, there was no change in expenditure on labor market programs between 2009 and 2018 as a percentage of GDP per capita (ADB 2022b). According to the analysis, labor market programs are underutilized in the region.

29 ILO. Strategies for Youth Employment. Employment Policy Gateway.

The depth in provision of labor market programs, as well as the breadth of their population coverage, varies deeply.[30] Rates of coverage as a share of target beneficiaries vary from 10.0% in Singapore, 6.6% in the Republic of Korea, and 6.4% in Cambodia—to less than 0.1% in Nepal and Indonesia (ADB 2022b). While there is no youth-specific breakdown of spending (Box 6), an important finding highlighted the need to consider new ways to include the "missing middle"[31] in social protection. Reaching them is essential, particularly in the recovery from the COVID-19 pandemic. Job matching can play an important role in the policy mix.

Box 6

The Youth Employment Evidence Gap in Asia and the Pacific

Evidence about the effectiveness of youth employment programs has been growing, but significant gaps remain. As shown in Box 5, blended interventions that combine multiple support types (e.g., skills training, job matching, and entrepreneurship financing) work best, yet how to tailor packages for different profiles of young people needs more research.

There are particular geographic deficits in the youth employment evidence base, with interventions in Asia and the Pacific relatively understudied. A seminal systematic review on youth employment reported limited information on South Asia, East Asia, the Pacific, and the Arab States and North Africa. A follow-up evidence gap map, including studies until January 2020, found that most randomized control trials of youth employment programs were conducted in Sub-Saharan Africa, followed by the Americas. Addressing the youth employment evidence gap in the Asia and Pacific region will better equip policy and program stakeholders to allocate scarce resources more effectively.

Sources: Kluve et al. (2017); Apunyo et al. (2022).

[30] Depth represents the average value of the benefits received by each beneficiary as a share of GDP per capita. Breadth represents the number of beneficiaries relative to the total target beneficiaries.

[31] The "missing middle" refers to people who are ineligible for contributory social insurance schemes—which account for a large share of expenditure—and are not covered by public social assistance and labor market policies. These people tend to be informal workers, youth, women, migrant workers, and other vulnerable groups.

SIRIUS
49-B1
319.13

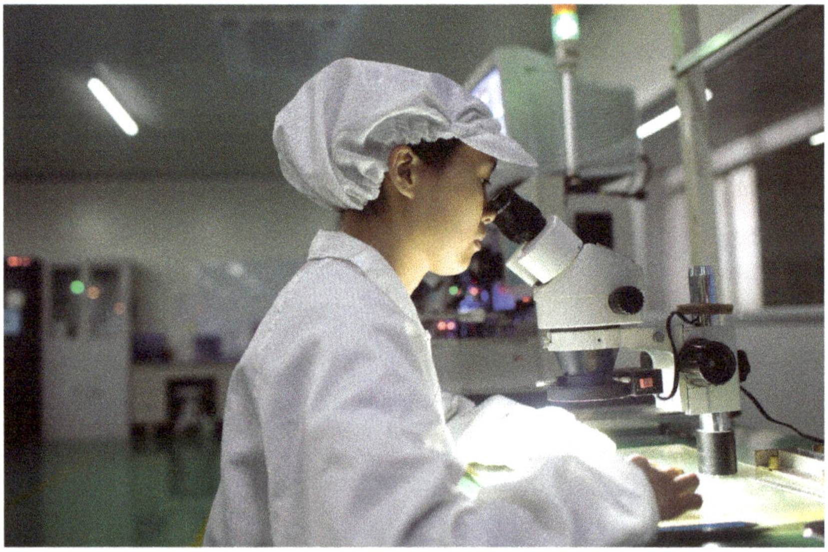

4

REVIEW OF YOUTH JOB-MATCHING MODELS IN ASIA AND THE PACIFIC

This chapter reviews 31 youth job-matching models from 13 countries in Asia and the Pacific. Only models that include direct job placement or employer connection services for youth are included. Key design and delivery features are highlighted to provide practical insights into the operation of job-matching services by governments, the private sector, and civil society. Four factors are defined that determine approaches of youth job-matching programs.

Job-matching services have proliferated over the last decade in Asia and the Pacific. At the same time, the various support services for youth employment have also expanded. At the intersection of these two trends is an increase in youth job-matching services. It is useful to take stock of these services and to unpack their design and delivery features, with a view to showcasing innovation and highlighting diversity. Doing so will not only help address the knowledge gap in this field but also provide useful insights for the design of new programs and the reform of existing ones.

This chapter presents a review of 31 youth job-matching models. These models were selected by canvassing (i) job-matching models for all ages and including only those with a focus on youth, and (ii) youth employment support programs that include job matching but may have been overlooked in (i). As set out earlier in the report, job matching means active support to place young people into available employment. Only models that include this support were reviewed in this report; programs that only provide job seeker preparation or search assistance were not. Some job-matching programs do provide or are linked to preparation and search services. As such, the links with these other services are discussed, as they are often integral to job matching (Figure 8).

Figure 8: Scope of Models Reviewed by Type of Intermediation Support

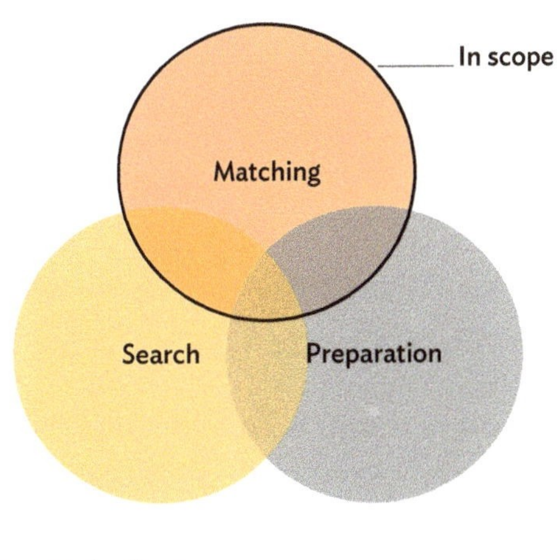

Source: Authors.

> Job matching means active support to place young people into available employment. Only models that include this support were reviewed in this report; programs that only provide job seeker preparation or search assistance were not.

Models were also selected to showcase innovation and to highlight stakeholder and country diversity (Box 7). Models were included that illustrate features or practices that can provide lessons for other countries and areas, programs, and/or stakeholders. As the selection includes programs headed by governments, the private sector, and nonprofit sector, it allows for a comparison of their differences, including funding. Finally, an effort was made to represent all subregions and a variety of countries. As a result, the 31 models are drawn from 13 countries (Table 1). The five selection criteria—job matching, youth, innovation, stakeholders, and country diversity—are set out in Box 7.

Table 1: Job-Matching Models Reviewed

Dimension	No.
No. of job-matching models	31
No. of countries in the Asia and Pacific region	13
No. of subregions in Asia and the Pacific	5
No. of categories of youth job-matching models	6

No. = number.

Source: Authors.

Two-thirds of the job-matching models were initiated in or after 2015. This suggests growth in the number of programs in recent years. All models were started during the 2000s, except one established in 1998 in the Republic of Korea.

Box 7

Criteria for Selecting Models

From among (all) job-matching models, those selected:

1. **Target youth** as users and beneficiaries, with a focus on vulnerable youth (e.g., disadvantaged groups, including rural youth, young people with disabilities).

From among youth employment support programs, those selected:

2. **Provide matching services** as a key support service, either as a stand-alone service, linked to other services, or as part of a larger support package.

From the youth job-matching services identified under 1 and 2, those selected:

3. **Highlight innovation and learning** by providing insights into leading practices for learning and replication by other countries;
4. **Represent stakeholder diversity,** illustrating the roles of public, private, and nonprofit stakeholders; and
5. **Represent country and area diversity,** drawn from across the Asia and Pacific region.

Source: Authors.

4.1 Categorization of Youth Job Matching

The review defined six categories of youth job-matching models in the region (Figure 9).

Figure 9: Categorization of Youth Job-Matching Models in Asia and the Pacific

- A Government Online Portals
- B Targeted Government Programs
- C Commercial Digital Platforms (for-profit)
- D Targeted Social Impact Models
- E Digital Bootcamps
- F Multistakeholder Partnerships (corporate-funded)

Source: Authors.

Each category is illustrated by four to five examples. The exception is commercial digital platforms, which has eight examples, highlighting its proliferation. Table 2 presents the models by category and includes the country and launch year.

Table 2: Youth Job-Matching Models Selected for Review

Model	Lead Country	Launch Year	Key Features
CATEGORY A: GOVERNMENT ONLINE PORTALS			
Work-Net	Republic of Korea	1998	• One-stop portal for labor market data, career information, and employment policies • AI-based job matching • Customized youth support available, Work-Net-for-Youth
National Career Service (NCS)	India	2015	• Centralized online career and job-matching platform • Aggregator of job-matching sites • Focused on youth
MyCareersFuture	Singapore	2018	• Smart job search and career advice platform • "Job-to-skills" job-matching technology • For young job seekers, mid-career professionals, and mature workers
National Intelligence for Skills, Education, Employment and Entrepreneurship (NISE)	Bangladesh	2018	• Job search and skills training online ecosystem • Demand-led data analytics • Connects employers, training providers, government, and young people
Aatmanirbhar Skilled Employee–Employer Mapping (ASEEM)	India	2020	• AI-based directory of the skilled workforce • Labor market data analytics • Connects employers, training partners, government, and young people

continued on next page

Table 2: *Continued*

Model	Lead Country	Launch Year	Key Features
CATEGORY B: TARGETED GOVERNMENT PROGRAMS			
JobStart Philippines	Philippines	2011	• Full-cycle youth employment facilitation program • Training and internship • Targeted at low-income NEET youth
Deen Dayal Upadhyaya Grameen Kaushalya Yojana (DDU-GKY)	India	2014	• Rural-training and job-matching program • Job placement in wage employment • Targeted at marginalized youth in poverty
Work-Study Certificate	Singapore	2015	• Government-sponsored training and hiring scheme • Matching in wage employment in field of study • Targeted at new graduates
Skills and Employability Enhancement Project	Tajikistan	2020–2027	• ADB-funded project for skills development and job matching • Priority sectors: tourism, agriculture, and energy • Targeted at youth, women, and labor migrants
Urban Youth Employment Project II	Papua New Guinea	2020–2025	• Second-phase IDA investment project for training, public works, and job matching • Job placement and referral service • Targeted at youths who have been out of work and out of school for at least 6 months
CATEGORY C: COMMERCIAL DIGITAL PLATFORMS			
Glints	Singapore, Southeast Asia	2015	• Online career discovery and job-matching platform • Smart job search and bootcamp programs • Targeted at young professionals
JobHopin	Viet Nam	2016	• Online job search and recruitment platform • First platform powered by AI and machine learning in Viet Nam • Targets interns and new graduates as well as more experienced workers
MyRobin	Indonesia	2019	• Mobile job-matching platform • Complementary access to financial services and other performance-related benefits • Targeted at blue-collar and entry-level roles
Apna	India	2019	• Mobile platform for job-matching and career guidance • With social networking and upskilling • Targeted at blue-collar and low-skilled job seekers including new graduates
BDjobs.com	Bangladesh	2000	• Online job-matching platform • With e-learning platform • Popular among low-income youth for skilled professions and vocational trades

continued on next page

Table 2: *Continued*

Model	Lead Country	Launch Year	Key Features
Green Collar	Singapore	2020	• Job-matching platform specializing in green jobs • Job search only • Targets students and first-time job seekers as well as mid-career professionals
BrightMinds	Singapore	n.d.	• Online job-matching portal • Automated search for job seekers and employers • For tertiary graduates to find their first jobs
Firstnaukri.com	India	n.d.	• Online job-matching platform • With career guidance services • Targeted exclusively at campus hiring for graduates into entry-level jobs
CATEGORY D: TARGETED SOCIAL IMPACT MODELS			
Digital Divide Data	Cambodia, Lao PDR, Kenya	2001	• Data-preparation services firm • Impact-sourcing model for training and hiring • Targeted at underserved communities including disadvantaged youth
Virtualahan	Philippines	2015	• Social enterprise virtual school • Training and job placement • Targeted at people with disabilities, NEET youth, and other marginalized groups
Generation	Pakistan, India, global	2015	• Nonprofit multistakeholder initiative by McKinsey in 17 countries • Training and job matching in high-demand sectors • Targeted at disadvantaged job seekers, both entry-level and mid-career
Enablecode	Viet Nam	2015	• Social enterprise for digital work • Digital skills training and job placement in outsourced ICT work • Exclusively for youth with disabilities
SwarajAbility	India	2022	• First AI-based job portal for people with disabilities in India • Training and online job matching • Run by a youth education and employment NGO, Youth4Jobs Foundation
CATEGORY E: DIGITAL BOOTCAMPS			
General Assembly	Singapore	2011	• International bootcamp provider in digital careers • Job-placement support and services for employers • Focus on youth
Hacktiv8	Indonesia	2016	• Coding bootcamp • Job-placement support and hiring portal for partner employers • Targeted at youth

continued on next page

Table 2: *Continued*

Model	Lead Country	Launch Year	Key Features
Eskwelabs	Philippines, Southeast Asia programs	2019	• Online digital-upskilling school • Apprenticeships and guaranteed job interviews with hiring partners • Targeted at youth
FunctionUp	India	2021	• Pay-after-placement bootcamp • 100% job guarantee with registered employers • For students in their final years of school or who have graduated within 3 years
CATEGORY F: CORPORATE-FUNDED MULTISTAKEHOLDER PARTNERSHIPS			
REACH	Viet Nam	2008	• Global program by Credit Suisse through 74 partners • Projects aim to close the education-to-employment gap for youth • Includes a vocational training and job placement model
Global Opportunity Youth Network (GOYN)	India	2019	• Global multistakeholder coalition convened by Aspen Institute • Promotes place-based youth economic inclusion approaches • Includes a model in India featuring job placement activities
Young Futuremakers	Thailand, Malaysia, Global	2019–2023	• Global initiative in 35 countries by Standard Chartered • Youth economic inclusion projects across education, employability, and entrepreneurship • Includes job-placement program components in Thailand and Malaysia
Pathways to Progress II	India, Bangladesh, Regional/ Global	2020–2023; since 2014	• $100-million global initiative by Citi and Citi Foundation • Projects to build job skills and to increase economic opportunity for youth • Includes in India and Bangladesh with job placement support

ADB = Asian Development Bank; AI = artificial intelligence; ICT = information and communication technology; IDA = International Development Association; Lao PDR = Lao People's Democratic Republic; NEET = not in employment, education, or training; NGO = nongovernment organization.

Notes:

1. See Appendix 1 for sources for these models.
2. Data on impact or reach are not included due to lack of consistency about indicator definitions and reporting. For example, some online job-matching platforms may record historical data on the volume of registered job seekers; others may share numbers of active users.
3. Data on beneficiary numbers or other data on reach and impact included in this chapter are from January to March 2023.

The 31 models can be assessed along four parameters. These parameters highlight the differences in design and operational approaches of youth job matching. They cover the key considerations of whom a model serves, what it offers, and how it is delivered (i.e., through which stakeholders and modality). How youth job-matching support is provided is often as important as what is provided. The four parameters are:

(i) **Profile of youth.** The job-matching program may cater to all youth or focus on one or multiple cohorts of youth. These cohorts can be based on family background, location, level of education and skills, or work and life experiences. Targeting a specific youth cohort can help tailor the type, intensity, and timing of support to ensure quality job matches.

(ii) **Range of services.** Models vary by the extent to which matching is linked with or includes related services. Matching can be a standalone service; it can be linked to job preparation services or job search support, or it can be part of a larger package of youth employment support.

(iii) **Type of provider.** Job-matching services can be provided by the public, private, or nonprofit sector. They can also be provided through partnerships or networks among these three types of providers. Models can be delivered at the local, subnational, national, or regional level.[32]

(iv) **Modality of delivery.** The way services are delivered to youth is another important factor. Many programs are primarily or entirely digital; others retain a nondigital, in-person approach to providing services. Programs may also combine or blend digital and nondigital services.

The 31 models represent different applications of the parameters. They cover a mix of youth-only and youth-inclusive models. They differentiate job-matching-centric models from broader models where matching is one service among others. They distinguish between government and private sector approaches. They specify digital and partly digital approaches. The four parameters are used to organize the findings of the review that follows (Figure 10).

Figure 10: Four Parameters That Define Youth Job-Matching Models

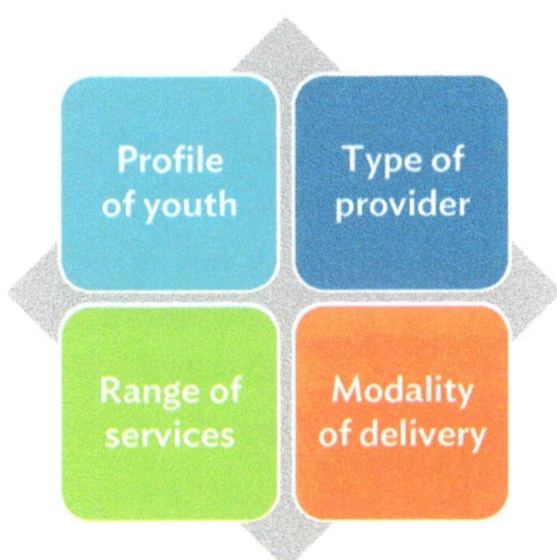

Source: Authors.

[32] Some models aim to improve labor mobility through intra- or inter-country migration, but these are not studied in this report.

4.2 Delivery Features

In this section, practical insights about youth job-matching models are discussed in detail. The features of the 31 models are assessed according to the four parameters that shape the youth job-matching landscape (Figure 10). For example, the first parameter may analyze the targeting approach of a model, the third parameter focuses on the contributions of different stakeholders, and the fourth parameter sets out its modality of delivery. In practice, the four factors are interlinked. The profiles of young people can determine the combination of services needed, how they are most appropriately delivered, as well as which type of stakeholders are best placed to provide support. These factors, as an organizing framework, enable careful examination of operational features that can generate insights for policymakers and stakeholders. Linkages between the findings of different factors are highlighted. The factors cannot only be used to analyze how a model works but also applied ex-ante to help improve the design and implementation of models.

Parameter 1: Profile of Youth

The different ways of targeting youth is a key design factor of job-matching models. The main difference is between models that serve only youth (i.e., youth-only) and those that include both youth and adult job seekers (i.e., youth-inclusive). For youth-only models, some cater broadly to all youth, while others target specific youth cohorts, including vulnerable groups. Youth-inclusive models have youth-relevant features.

Some models solely target youth. Across all types of job-matching models, a significant share are designed only for youth. These youth-only models tend to be based on deep knowledge of youth's needs and aspirations regarding entering the labor market, securing first jobs, and navigating the early phases of their careers. Sixteen of the 31 models reviewed are youth-only. In addition, many models tend to specialize in a particular subgroup of youth. These can include tertiary graduates who may face an industry skills mismatch, or marginalized young people who need an intensive mix of support.

> The commercial jobs matching platform Glints was launched in Singapore by its young founders as an informal service among friends to find internships. It has since expanded to Indonesia; Malaysia; Philippines; Taipei,China; and Viet Nam, helping young professionals (i.e., those ages 16–26 years) discover their career paths and find jobs. It continues to offer access to internships as well as other employment options for young workers and job seekers, including part-time and project-based positions. The platform allows users to filter vacancies by years of experience, including a youth-friendly category requiring less than 1 year of experience. It has placed more than 4 million job seekers.[33]

> In India, the established online jobs site Naukri.com spun off a youth-targeted site, Firstnaukri.com. Aimed at tertiary graduates, it helps them find their first jobs or internships. It provides a range of career guidance services tailored to the needs of graduates, including curriculum vitae development

[33] Glints.

and first-time interview preparation. Users can navigate job preparation support by study area or graduation year. In 2022, over 45,000 graduates were placed into work through a network of more than 5,000 employers and 8,000 campuses.[34]

A different approach is taken by the Global Opportunity Youth Network (GOYN), a multistakeholder coalition seed funded by Prudential Financial and housed at the Aspen Institute in Washington, DC.[35] The model targets young people (i.e., those ages 15–29 years) who are out of school, unemployed, or in informal jobs. Networks are created that bring together young people with local governments, businesses, skilling partners, and others. Nine locations—including three in Asia—were selected in 2018 for the first wave of activity. In Pune, India, the local GOYN program allows youth to apply for skills and job placement support in a range of in-demand positions, such as 3D printing machine operators and installers and advanced CCTV camera installers.

Other models in the region support youth within a broader pool of job seekers. Young people are also served by job-matching models that are not exclusively targeted at youth. Instead, they cater to young job seekers as part of a wider target audience (i.e., they are intentionally inclusive of youth). Some approaches intentionally streamline support by enabling job seekers to navigate based on their profiles. In some models, youth are targeted among other groups, such as female job seekers, migrant workers (whose citizenship status may affect eligibility for certain jobs), or older workers (who face displacement from their jobs due to age or obsolete skills or who want to work beyond normal retirement age). Fifteen out of the 31 models reviewed target youth as part of a broader offering.

In the Republic of Korea, the government's online job-matching platform, WorkNet, serves all job seekers. However, it features a dedicated section for youth, Work-Net-For-Youth, that posts job opportunities targeted at first-time or early-career workers. Resources are customized and user-friendly for youth. For example, training content is provided in video format; advice and job opportunities are available from smaller firms who are major employers of youth; and guidance is geared to first-time job seekers, such as for submitting applications for the first time or preparing for first interviews. The site is easy to navigate from online career service systems of universities. On the main WorkNet site, 10 of the 23 vocational aptitude and psychological tests are designed for youth for their self-assessment. WorkNet also has dedicated sections for older persons, women, and other groups in the labor market.

The Government of Singapore's online job portal, MyCareersFuture, divides users into three groups by career stage: (i) youth (i.e., new entrants and new graduates), (ii) mid-career professionals, and (iii) mature workers. Job matching for youth is based on skills, past applications, and past searches, with less emphasis on work experience. Young job seekers can also find less-competitive vacancies through a search function that differentiates between "job roles that need more applications" and "job roles with many applications."

34 Firstnaukri.com.

35 GOYN's other partners include Global Development Incubator, YouthBuild International, and Accenture.

A popular commercial job-matching site in Bangladesh, BDJobs.com, serves a broad range of job seekers across skilled professions and vocational trades (e.g., electricians or drivers). The site normally has over 16,000 vacancies available from some 2,500 companies. Informal workers and low-income youth are part of its targeting. Jobs can be filtered by age range, including under age 20 years as well as ages 20–30 years, and by experience, including under 1 year as well as 1–3 years. Vacancies include work-from-home, contractual, and part-time work. A new feature on the site is a section for jobs for "freshers" (i.e., recent graduates).

Some models focus on a specific group of youth—especially vulnerable youth. Typically, these models have multiple components, linking to personalized preparation support (e.g., counseling or mentoring) so that the needs and aspirations of these young people can be understood and addressed. There is a strong focus in the region on supporting youth with disabilities, in which addressing spatial and other access constraints as well as discriminatory employer perceptions are important. Low-income and inactive youth are another priority target group. Here, effective outreach is needed, and peer-to-peer engagement and civil society partnership can be useful mechanisms. The review only identified two models for rural youth.

A job-matching model that targets youth with disabilities is Enablecode in Viet Nam. It partners with the United Nations Children's Fund (UNICEF) and various disability-focused civil society organizations to identify potential job seekers. At the pre-matching stage, it provides comprehensive training to prepare these youth for work. Digital skills training through Amazon's cloud computing program is combined with personal development and work readiness training. The training is inspired by Maslow's hierarchy of needs spanning basic needs and self-fulfillment. Training graduates are placed with business process outsourcing firms and other business partners. While impact data are not available, Enablecode is seeking to reach 100,000 young people.[36]

Turning to geographic targeting, the Government of India has provided a training and job placement scheme for poor rural youth since 2014. Deen Dayal Upadhyaya Grameen Kaushalya Yojana (DDU-GKY) targets young people in poverty ages 15–35 years living in rural communities. To date, over 760,000 young people have been placed in jobs out of some 1.25 million trained.[37] Further targeting prioritizes youth from tribal groups, youth with disabilities, and marginalized women. Life, digital, and technical skills training are provided for 584 job types across 52 subsectors. Youth are provided with free accommodation, meals, and travel stipends. They may also be supported to obtain biometric identification cards and bank accounts.

NEET youth are the target of a program in Papua New Guinea jointly provided by the government and World Bank. The Urban Youth Employment Project II targets NEET youth ages 16–29 years who have been out of school and out of work for at least 6 months.

36 Enablecode.

37 Deen Dayal Upadhyaya Grameen Kaushalya Yojana.

Implemented by the National Capital District Commission, the project delivers a sequenced support package that combines training and work experience to prepare youth for work. A public works component also provides experience and bolsters awareness of the world of work for hard-to-engage youth. Job matching is provided through 3-month internships that can lead to regular jobs. In the project's first phase, two-thirds of youth who completed on-the-job training were offered jobs by these employers (World Bank, 2020).

Targeting by skills and education level is a common approach. Another targeting mechanism common in job matching is to tailor services by a young person's level of skills or formal education. These are directly aligned with the required qualifications in job vacancies. In particular, the review found a range of schemes available based on graduation from a particular type of education institution. Such models aim to address the needs of job-seeking graduates as well as employers seeking to recruit qualified youth.

The Government of Singapore's Work-Study Certificate targets graduates of the Institute of Technical Education, polytechnical school, and national (i.e., military) service. Youth within 3 years of graduation are eligible to apply. They are matched to quality jobs related to their fields of study within a network of participating employers across sectors. They undergo 12–18-month programs that include instruction, on-the-job training, work projects, and supervision by workplace mentors. Upon completion, they receive industry-recognized certificates. If they perform well, they may be offered full-time employment. The scheme provides a mechanism for employers to find and to groom suitable talent and for job seekers to enter the world of work.

The Aatamanirbhar Skilled Employee Employer Mapping (ASEEM) platform, launched by the Government of India in 2020, takes a different approach to improving the entry of skilled youth into the world of work. It hosts a national directory of available skilled workers, with an aim to improve youth livelihoods. Workers are mapped and then matched at a hyper-local level by skills level to job vacancies. The platform is integrated with government-skilling schemes to facilitate a single interface for the skills development of youth and skills-based hiring. User profiles for the service can be generated from data already stored in the Skill India Portal or from labor migration programs.

The commercial job-matching platform FunctionUp in India supplies work-ready youth to leading technology companies. It targets tertiary students in their final school years and those who graduated within the past 3 years. It is designed to kickstart careers in software development and to bridge the gap between youth job seekers and over 1,000 ICT companies. It is an official partner of the National Skill Development Council (NSDC). Intensive training courses are also designed in collaboration with employer partners to ensure that these youth are prepared for the targeted jobs.

A range of strategies help improve inclusivity of job-matching models. The review found that programs not specifically designed to cater to particular at-risk groups still adopt strategies to expand their access to disadvantaged youth. For example, models that primarily cater to educated youth (i.e., who can often afford to pay fees) also run schemes to enable participation of low-income or low-skilled youth. Some job-matching models offer income-linked scholarships or the option to delay fee payments until after employment is secured. Complementing job matching with basic life skills and job readiness training also helps level the playing field for disadvantaged youth. Gender-based strategies help increase the labor market access and retention of young women. Making mainstream services accessible to people with disabilities is also an important part of improving inclusivity.

Hactiv8 is a coding bootcamp in Indonesia that offers a study-now-pay-later scheme to expand access to certain types of employment for low-income youth. Participants are supported by a job placement team to secure work with a network of over 750 employers. Course fees are paid through installments after graduation, typically over 2–3 years; women are given a 10% discount on fees. Repayment amounts vary according to salaries. Full- and part-time courses are available. A guarantee provides a payout if trainees do not find employment within 4 months. Educational background is not an admissions criterion. Psychological counseling is available for less-confident youth.

The Skills and Employability Enhancement Project in Tajikistan is designed to expand job market access for young women. The project is funded by ADB and the Government of Japan and implemented by the Government of Tajikistan. Specialist job centers will be built for the tourism, agriculture, and energy sectors to service job seekers in these sectors. Services at these centers will include job counseling and matching to link the interests and skills of job seekers with local vacancies. Free childcare will be provided, and women will be offered stipends for training courses. Individual and family counseling will also be available. The centers will work with business groups to increase female employment in the energy sector.

Online jobs platform BDJobs.com in Bangladesh provides a website and services that are accessible for people with disabilities. It follows Web Content Accessibility Guidelines and provides links to assistive technologies, such as screen readers. As well as providing support to job seekers with disabilities, BDJobs.com provides a range of disability-related services to employers, including sensitizing businesses on providing an inclusive workplace, systems, and policies; building an inclusive talent pipeline; and providing training and resources on disability inclusion.

Models have different ways to understand the individual profile of the young user to strengthen targeting and to personalize support. As discussed earlier in the report, youth employment support is shifting to customize provision to the individual needs of each young person. The job-matching models reviewed in the region illustrate the different approaches to profiling youth and to adapting support based on their specific characteristics. An interesting change is how young people can better build their profiles, moving beyond formal qualifications and work experience. Across the wave of new online job-matching offerings, a range of digital assessment and profiling tools are catering to target groups to define and to assess their skills, competences, and experiences in a way that improves their employability and helps communicate their fit with a particular vacancy.[38] Offline, some models employ career coaches, counselors, and mentors who work one-on-one or with small groups of youth. Through dialogue, they help young people identify and articulate what they offer the job market and how they can strengthen their profiles.

Virtualahan is a virtual school in the Philippines that trains young people with disabilities in digital skills and places them into work. Job and life coaching are used to diagnose factors that influence each person's employability and to provide tailored support. Participants join in well-being sessions to build dignity and emotional intelligence that is critical to thrive in life and the workplace. A detailed employment and psychological profile of the participant is built through coaching and can be used to provide guidance to an employer about the attributes of a potential recruit, including any specific needs. It has trained over 1,000 youth and has a job placement rate of 69%.[39]

The blue-collar worker platform MyRobin in Indonesia illustrates the growing use of digital professional profiling. Workers are profiled based on experience, skills, location, and other factors relevant to obtaining a job. A digital profiling tool is used to create profiles similar to those used on LinkedIn, which include structured logs of work completed that record skills and experience gained. This helps demonstrate each person's suitability for a job and identify skills deficiencies to pursue re-/upskilling. An online database of close to 3 million profiled workers is available to registered employers.

In 2018, the Government of Bangladesh launched the National Intelligence for Skills, Education, Employment and Entrepreneurship (NISE), a skills and training platform that connects employers, training providers, and young job seekers. It provides job search as well as profiling and assessment tools to help youth understand the skills and other assets that they can offer employers—especially if they have only limited formal education, training, or work experience. There are filters and directions for youth facing constraints so that they can access tailored services. For example, youth in remote rural areas can access migration services.

Parameter 2: Range of Services

Another variable determining youth job-matching approaches is the extent to which matching is the core service or ancillary. Some models are established to strengthen matching between young job seekers and employers. These models typically offer complementary job search and preparation services. Moreover, there is a growing focus on providing value to employers as well as to job seekers through combining matching with other workforce development services. The review identified job matching within much broader youth livelihood programs (i.e., models that incorporate other support types beyond intermediation support, such as skills training or self-employment support).

38 More discussion on technology improving user profiling is covered under Parameter 4.

39 Virtualahan.

Many models are developed with a focus on improving the matching of young job seekers with employers. Job matching is the primary function of these models, such as government online platforms and commercial digital platforms. They strengthen the transaction between employers and job seekers. A significant enabler of market growth is the digitalization of services, as discussed under Parameter 4, and as reflected in the categorization of models (Figure 9). Online platforms also create a space to search for candidates and jobs and may provide preparation services, as discussed further. Some models broker the employer–job seeker connection offline. Others combine skills training to expand opportunities for more young people.

Platforms like JobsCentral BrightMinds in Singapore exist primarily to connect youth with employers for work. They seek to be a trusted space for youth to search for and to secure employment. They aim to ease the job search and application process, making it more likely that youth will engage in active searches, make good use of their time, and find suitable employment. A large and diverse pool of employers attractive to young job seekers helps drive uptake. Support is also provided to employers to reduce their hiring costs.

Social impact models like Digital Divide Data in Cambodia help rectify the exclusion of disadvantaged youth working in the technology sector by focusing on upskilling and matching them to quality jobs. The network of organizations across industries that partner with Digital Divide Data is central to the employment opportunities available. These organizations trust this talent pipeline and are thus motivated to diversify their workforce through inclusion of young people who they would struggle to reach and to hire independently.

The Government of Singapore added the Work-Study Certificate to its labor market program tool kit to address worsening problems within graduate recruitment across industries. The scheme is designed to place target cohorts into quality work, helping address the skills gap. Engaging the private sector in training curriculum design is now common in many countries and areas, yet the Work-Study Certificate scheme deepens this partnership. Through the scheme, firms and the government enter a cost-sharing arrangement to improve recruitment and labor market outcomes of educated youth in the country.

Complementary job preparation and skills development services improve matching and open up access for more youth. Job matching is often provided in some combination with job preparation and skills development. Matching will only be successful if youth are job ready. Given a low level of employability among youth, upskilling young job seekers can pay large dividends when they look for work. This means addressing technical skills gaps as well as life and soft skills gaps. For models targeting more job-ready youth, support focuses on job preparation, including, for example, curriculum vitae development and preparation for aptitude testing and interviews.

The Government of Singapore developed Workipedia as an integral part of its MyCareersFuture portal. Designed as a one-stop site for career-related resources to achieve a quality job match, support focuses on developing skills for job searches as well as career development. Users are guided to relevant career events, training courses, and other government services. Articles and tools are available as well, segmented by career stage.

As part of the Glints job portal in Singapore, Glints ExpertClass offers a program of mainly fee-based classes that support youth in exploring their potential and improving their job skills and competencies. They provide alternative pathways into work for youth. Classes are run by industry experts and cover a range of technical and personal development topics. They range from intensive programs over 8 weeks to one-off webinars and workshops. Classes are developed in collaboration with various industries.

Through its corporate citizenship program Future Skills, Credit Suisse supports REACH, a nongovernment organization in Viet Nam. It places disadvantaged youth into permanent employment with employer partners. First, target youth must complete a comprehensive training program, which addresses their lack of formal education. Trainees can select 3–6-month courses from in-demand sectors. These sectors are identified through market analysis, and courses are developed in collaboration with industry. A nine-step training approach covers English language as well technical and soft skills training.

Building a job seeker profile is a growing service area that improves job matching. Formal qualifications and clarity in communicating value to a prospective employer can create distinct advantages for job seekers. Yet, this can entrench disadvantages for youth with lower levels of formal education, certified skills, or workplace awareness. The review identified a trend across models for alternative products and services that help inexperienced and poorly qualified youth build and communicate their employment profiles. This can incorporate tools to assess and to address skills gaps, processes to document skills and experiences gained through work, and alternative resume builders. As with other innovations in job matching, technology is opening new opportunities for automating and digitizing profiles (Parameter 4).

The job-matching app Apna in India caters to a target audience of informal workers with low skills and education. These job seekers do not typically have experience or awareness of how best to communicate with potential employers. A profile-builder tool on the platform, however, allows users to document their value and interests in a consistent format and to connect with relevant employers. This is likely to be the only opportunity that these users have to build their digital professional identities. Once personal information is entered, a profile in the form of a virtual business card that serves as a resume is created and then matched to relevant employers.

BDjobs.com in Bangladesh has developed an employability assessment test through a joint venture with Aspiring Minds' Computer Adaptive Test. This industry-recognized certification test produces a detailed report including score, personality and job-fit insights, recommended jobs and sectors in which to seek work, and guidance to improve employability. After completing the test, rates of resume views, interviews, and job matches increase.[40]

Gamified assessment is simplifying job application on recruitment platform JobHopin in Viet Nam. This is enabling a broader range of youth to demonstrate their knowledge and skills, including those with limited formal qualifications or experience to share.

[40] BDjobs.com.

Assessments take the form of user-friendly youth-targeted quizzes, which help young users assess their skills, identify their skills gaps, and upgrade their knowledge. Employers can also tailor assessments to their corporate priorities and evaluate important psychological characteristics through this approach.

Facilitating access to social networks is another service that complements job matching. Referrals and word of mouth remain key channels for job hunting at all skills levels. The dynamics of these processes depend on context. For educated youth, alumni can provide a valuable support network and source of opportunities and recommendations in the job market, especially from prestigious institutions. In low-income contexts with weak infrastructure and mainly informal employment, job search and recruitment also tend to be informal through information from friends, relatives, and peers in the same trade. Youth job-matching models are incorporating various ways to include the experience and possibilities of social networks (with a role for digital networks as covered in Parameter 4).

Apna in India aims to recreate the offline social networks common among informal workers by building "vertical professional communities." There are more than 70 communities categorized by trade, including for carpenters, electricians, and delivery people. These communities are spaces for like-minded and similarly skilled people to connect, share tips, and exchange job experiences and opportunities. Apna is growing as a three-part model to maximize the impact of its job-matching component through a vocational social network, jobs marketplace, and upskilling.

Online jobs site JobsCentral BrightMinds in Singapore introduced a referral program for employers, recognizing the key role that current employees play in finding new hires. CareerBuilder's SocialReferral tool allows companies to ask employees to act as social referral ambassadors to identify potential applicants for jobs. They are rewarded for sharing job postings on their personal networks and recommending candidates for vacancies. It claims that it is 55% faster to identify and to hire candidates referred by employees and that they are 13% more likely to stay for the long term.[41]

At online school Eskwelabs in the Philippines, learning is delivered in groups or cohorts to facilitate peer-to-peer support and networking. Making the learning experience social helps build critical life skills through teamwork and collaboration, which are directly applicable to the workplace. Trainees establish relationships with peers that are sustained post-program and can provide labor market support and information. Eskwelabs works to nurture the sense of belonging for each cohort to maximize community benefits.

Post-placement support can help strengthen job matching, and provision varies. Continued support for young people after they secure a job will increase the likelihood that they can perform well in their jobs, maximize their potential, and pursue quality onward transitions. Some models consider job placement the end of the process; others have a longer-term lens and provide post-placement support

41 CareerBuilder. An Introduction to SocialReferral.

to help youth stay in their jobs. It is common for young workers to bounce out of first jobs, creating a need for job-matching support to focus both on the quality of first jobs as well as on those who need to find new jobs.

Online site JobHopin in Viet Nam is an example of the many job-matching platforms that support the transaction of securing a job but do not follow up with post-placement support. Two types of subscriptions for employers indicate a focus on job placement; in neither case, however, do they pay to post vacancies. In the JobMatch package, employers are charged by the number of people who apply for a vacancy. Under JobHunt, employers pay when an offer is accepted. While post-placement support is not provided directly, JobHopin does play a role in building the wider start-up ecosystem by, for example, running enterprise challenges and co-hosting networking events.

In Credit Suisse's Future Skills partnership with REACH in Viet Nam, youth receive 6 months of support after they are placed in jobs. This ongoing engagement—typically through counseling—supports youth in settling into their workplaces and improves retention and performance. Surveying youth 6 months after placement generates valuable data about their transition experiences as well. Employer feedback also helps continuously enhance the model.

Job seekers using job-matching app MyRobin in Indonesia gain access to more support as their employment track record through the platform grows. They are incentivized to stay in employment and to work for job performance-related benefits, such as affordable vehicle leases and discounts on purchasing daily essentials (e.g., motorbike oil) through the platform. This brings value to employers by reducing turnover and increasing productivity. The model is designed to retain users who juggle multiple short-term and gig-based work placements. Opportunities for upskilling support access to better-quality work. As the platform grows, more financial services will become available for users.

Meeting the needs of employers is becoming more of a focus in youth job-matching models. Value provided through services for employers is increasingly a differentiator in the job-matching market. If an online portal starts as a simple vacancies board, the trend is for it to evolve to provide a broader array of services for youth as well as to support employers, such as through specialist search and recruitment services. As with job seekers, matching is often provided in combination with other types of support for employers and relates to all stages of onboarding, managing, and developing a workforce. If well supported, employers can reduce recruitment costs, improve the quality of hired talent, and increase retention, supporting better employment transitions for youth.

Graduate recruitment site Firstnaukri.com in India is designed to support employers, universities, and young graduates in the recruitment process. It aims to provide all of the information, resources, and support that employers need to identify, hire, and onboard graduates. It helps employers target specific campuses to find relevant candidates, depending on industry or sector. It also provides communications channels for employers to connect with students (e.g., email, voice mail, and SMS), market their company, and advertise vacancies. Online assessments are also incorporated for the screening and testing of candidates.

The government's NISE platform in Bangladesh provides employers with more than youth job matching. They can also access dashboards and data sets that provide insights into industry and labor market trends, helping forecast employers' future staff requirements. Via the platform, they are connected to training providers to define needs and access or to develop content for in-house training programs. NISE also works with the SME Foundation to increase access to the platform for cottage, micro, and SMEs, which are significant employers—especially of youth.

Hacktiv8 in Indonesia supports employers in developing in-house digital training programs. It runs 60 programs that can be used by different divisions of a company and adapted to a specific employer's needs. It supports firms' digital transformations, including talent planning, which can improve readiness for hiring, including of youth. Training extends to soft skills, including conflict management, emotional intelligence for leaders, and data-driven decision-making.

Job matching can be an additional component within a holistic youth livelihoods package. Holistic interventions for youth employment have emerged in recognition of evidence that integrated support works best. Youth—especially vulnerable ones—face multiple needs to prosper in the labor market, and different types of support can be bundled to address specific constraints—social, economic, or cultural. Job placement can be the later phase of a sequenced support package that takes them from disengagement in the labor market to job placement. Some initiatives are primarily skills focused but incorporate matching as a secondary component to improve the outcome of skills development.

The World Bank's Urban Youth Employment Project II in Papua New Guinea provides job placement of youth toward the end of a multistep livelihoods support program. The early stages of support are compulsory and intensive, in line with the distance that these young people are from being employable. They include basic life skills and job readiness training, 30 days of paid work in an urban works scheme, technical training, and internships. This is followed, at the last stage, by the matching of these youth into jobs.

Young FutureMakers is Standard Chartered's $75-million initiative to increase economic inclusion of disadvantaged youth. In its 2019–2023 program in Thailand, job placement is one part of a holistic program focused on youth who face additional social barriers to employment, such as gender or disabilities. Youth are matched to work-based learning and employment opportunities as part of a package of support including demand-led technical skills training, employability training, and career guidance. There are also activities to increase youth's awareness of labor rights and to improve employers' perceptions of the abilities and potential of disadvantaged youth and people with disabilities.

Citi Foundation's Pathways to Progress II projects are primarily skills-based. In Bangladesh, it ran a technical education program for underprivileged young women ages 17–25 years in collaboration with the nonprofit Underprivileged Children's Educational Program. Trainees received nationally certified training at technical schools in skills in high demand, including sewing and electronic assembly. Then, post-training, employment support services were provided to facilitate job matching and placement or self-employment.

Parameter 3: Type of Provider

Another key factor that defines youth job-matching models is the type of stakeholders involved. The public, private, and nonprofit sectors provide—or enable the provision of—job-matching services. In some models, provision is a collaborative effort among these different types of stakeholders. Following are the main findings, divided between the public and private sectors, with cross-references to nonprofit partners.

Public Sector

The public sector is a significant provider and enabler of job-matching services for youth, especially vulnerable youth. As identified in this review, governments may play one or more of four roles: providers of job-matching services; aggregators of information and job-matching support for youth; scaling partners to support expansion and replication of support; and financing partners to provide services, incentives, and other support.

Several governments in the region are leading the delivery of job-matching schemes for youth. Depending on the scope of decentralization of labor laws and the strategic goals of the schemes, job-matching schemes are led by various ministries and at different administrative levels. Government-led interventions are delivered online, offline, or both. They are well placed to deliver at scale and to reach vulnerable groups.

In Singapore, various schemes are led by different ministries and agencies. The public job-matching platform, MyCareersFuture, is delivered through a collaboration between the Government Technology Agency (GovTech) and Workforce Singapore, with the latter being under the Ministry of Manpower. This online service complements the government's offline career-matching services. Separately, SkillsFuture Singapore, under the Ministry of Education, runs the Work-Study Certificate scheme to prepare educated youth for the workforce. This certificate, as featured under Parameter 1, directly connects graduates to employment opportunities in their fields of study.

In the Philippines, JobStart is a government-run employment facilitation program for low-income NEET youth launched in 2011. The Department of Labor and Employment manages the program, which is administered through municipal public employment service offices. An oversight committee oversees implementation, chaired by the department and composed of representatives from the Department of the Interior and Local Government, National Youth Commission, Technical Education and Skills Development Authority, and others. The government partners with training institutes and employers to provide training and job matching. Nearly 30,000 young people have been trained, and more than 11,000 of these have been placed into jobs.[42]

[42] JobStart.

The DDU-GKY program for poor rural youth in India is led by the Ministry of Rural Development and is implemented at the state level. Youth access support at local training centers approved by sector skills councils of NSDC. NSDC is a nonprofit company structured as a public–private partnership, with the Ministry of Skill Development and Entrepreneurship holding 49% of the share capital and the private sector holding 51%. DDU-GKY partners with government training agencies and employers to train and to place youth in associated jobs.

Governments also play a central role in aggregating information and simplifying access to job-matching services for youth. This has become an increasingly valuable service with the proliferation of information and services online. The review found that government job-matching platforms not only aggregate job-matching sites in one place but increasingly provide links to complementary services provided by other parts of governments and the private sector. This also means that job-matching services can be bundled with other types of employment support services and labor market information. The digital aspects of aggregation through platforms are explored under Parameter 4.

The WorkNet platform in the Republic of Korea brings together 31 public and private job search websites, including services from the Ministry of Employment and Labor (Human Resources Development Service), Ministry of the Interior and Safety, Ministry of National Defence (Military Manpower Administration), and Ministry of Personnel Management. A one-stop shop for employment information and support, it aggregates a range of data and sources relating to all aspects of employment, from labor market policies to skills courses to job-matching and application support. It is operated by the Ministry of Employment and Labor and the Korea Employment Information Service.

The NISE platform in Bangladesh connects the job-matching ecosystem across employers, youth, and training providers. It brings together information from 32 government departments under 23 government ministries and 42 industry associations. It aggregates multiple data sources and produces and shares insights for users, covering all areas of employment including job forecasts, entrepreneurship support, and migration guidance. Job vacancies are aggregated for AI-enabled search by youth. NISE works through the government's public service innovation agency, Aspire to Innovate, which is led by the Information and Communication Technology Division, Ministry of Posts, Telecommunications, and Information Technology, in partnership with the government's Cabinet Division and the United Nations Development Programme.

In India, the government created the National Career Service in 2015 as a one-stop career and employment portal out of the reform and rationalization of previous disparate state-level employment exchanges. Run under the Ministry of Labour and Employment, the single national portal serves employers, job seekers, job employment organizations, training institutions, and career advisers. It brings together services across training, career counseling, and job matching. For job-matching services, some vacancies are posted directly on the platform, while others are aggregated from partner search and placement organizations. The platform makes clear if a vacancy is uploaded by a third party and names the partner. In these cases, users are navigated to the partner websites to continue the job application process.

Governments are the critical partner in scaling up job-matching models. Public sector legislation, regulation, administration, and infrastructure are very important in enabling national reach. Social impact job-matching models with no government engagement can lack the capacity needed to scale up. The review identified cases of government upscaling when the government is the lead implementer and when it is not. In models built on multistakeholder collaboration, the public sector—via national or local administration—can help embed delivery into the existing ecosystem and affect change at the system level. Some governments can also help replicate their good practices in other countries and areas through knowledge exchange.

The JobStart program in the Philippines was launched as a pilot project funded by ADB and the Government of Canada. It was tested in four local government units in 2014. Each unit had a target number of youth to support. Memorandums of understanding were signed between the Department of Labor and Employment and the mayors of the local government units. Following the pilot, legislation was enacted in 2016 for national implementation of the program, defining the duties and responsibilities of stakeholders and delivery entities. Today, JobStart is operational in almost 50 local government units, and a 5-year national roll-out strategy for 2022–2027 sets out plans for continued expansion, including more gender-sensitive implementation.

The jobs platform SwarajAbility in India shows how engaging government in a nongovernment initiative can strengthen market penetration and scaling. SwarajAbility is the first AI-powered jobs portal for people with disabilities in India—an innovative job-matching technology developed at the Indian Institute of Technology Hyderabad. Inputs were incorporated from a design and technology firm and a specialist youth and disabilities nongovernment organization that hosts the platform. The initiative was endorsed by the principal scientific adviser to the Government of India and launched in 2022.

Knowledge exchange is another mechanism that enables replication and scaling of good practices. The Government of the Republic of Korea is supporting developing countries to scale up their e-services for employment and to improve other associated policy areas. Its WorkNet platform supports South-South exchange based on the country's global leadership in e-governance. In particular, the Ministry of Employment and Labor has partnered with Cambodia to replicate WorkNet with the aim of creating a local employment service information portal. Support has also been provided to Mongolia, Sri Lanka, and Viet Nam to create digital networks for employment services.

Another key role for governments is financing youth job-matching programs. Funds are provided for the design and implementation of national programs and through allocations to local governments. Governments also partner with private intermediaries to provide financial incentives to deliver targeted support to youth. One such incentive is payment by results in terms of the number of job placements. Another approach is to provide grants to youth and/or employers to motivate engagement in job-matching schemes. Also, the cost of training and employing low-experience young workers can be defrayed through government subsidies.

In India, the government's job-matching scheme for poor rural youth, DDU-GKY, is designed to shift support away from only training youth to matching them into jobs or better jobs. As such, training partners are required to place at least 70% of graduates in jobs that pay a minimum salary of Rs6,000 ($72) per month. Once candidates are working, they receive post-placement financial support—the amount depends on whether they obtain jobs within the districts in which they live. If placed within their districts, monthly stipends of Rs1,000 ($12) are provided for 2 months. The period is extended to 3 months if the work is outside of their districts but within their states of residence and to 6 months if outside of their states. Employer partners are classified depending on how many candidates that they train and employ. If it is over 5,000 youth in 2 years, they are "Champion Employers;" if over 500 youth, they are "Captive Employers." The higher the number of young people hired, the better the partnership arrangements in terms of fast-tracked decisions and eligibility for cost-sharing arrangements with the government.

Singapore's Work-Study Certificate is another government program that provides financial incentives to both youth and employers. Eligible youth (i.e., Singapore citizens who are within 3 years of having graduated from partner institutions or completing military service) receive a sign-on incentive of S$5,000 ($3,660) when they join the scheme. Employers can receive grants per youth for mentoring (S$5,000), administration (S$2,000 [$1,460]), and on-the-job training and development of a blueprint for each unique job role (S$5,000). There is an additional on-the-job training grant for employers of S$15 ($11) per hour, capped at S$5,000 per trainee. If youth are placed in a job in an affiliate country, the employer can receive up to 90% of the costs of the overseas attachment, capped at S$8,000 ($5,850). During the COVID-19 pandemic, further wage assistance was provided to encourage retention and recruitment of youth. This assistance amounts were time-bound and higher for existing trainees, as companies hiring new trainees could qualify for other types of support.

The Government of the Philippines supports the costs of multiple program components of JobStart through grants to youth, employers, and training providers. For the first step in the program, the 10-day life skills training, youth receive ₱300 ($5) per day so that they can afford to attend the sessions. The next stage is technical training, which can be provided by a public employment services office, an employer, or a technical vocational institution. Grants are provided to these training partners, and trainees continue to receive a daily allowance of ₱300. For the internship, at least 75% of the minimum wage must be paid to interns by employers. To facilitate this, employers receive ₱1,500 ($26) per trainee each month for up to 6 months. This helps meet costs of administration, training, and development (i.e., an individualized training plan) for each youth. JobStart also pays for medical clearances before the internship and accident insurance for 12 months from the start of the life skills training.

Private Sector

The private sector has become increasingly engaged in providing job-matching services to youth. This review covered local commercial activity, multinational corporations (including philanthropy), and social enterprise. The nature of involvement depends on local contexts. A key variable is the quality and coverage of public sector provision, as the private sector can complement governments and open new opportunities.

Private sector models expand choice and competition in job-matching support for youth and employers. Ongoing barriers both to youth and to employers in the job search and matching process can be addressed by private solutions. In particular, the commercial sector of digital-based matching is growing, providing new ways for youth and employers to connect. Changing labor market dynamics have created opportunities for innovation provided by private providers as well. Models, such as bootcamps, focus on job preparation to strengthen digital skills, opening access to digital work. Such alternative pathways into in-demand sectors may be attractive to youth who have not obtained the requisite industry skills during their formal education. For technology companies, alternative models create a more workforce-ready cohort of youth.

In Singapore, BrightMinds is a recruitment platform for tertiary graduates. It is a youth-targeted spin-off from the company's main job-matching site, JobsCentral, illustrating the market opportunity of catering to the youth audience. Further, JobsCentral was acquired in 2011 by CareerBuilder, a human resources technology company in the United States. The global footprint of companies under the CareerBuilder umbrella across the life cycle of recruitment enables product innovation and market expansion at the Singapore affiliate.

Also, in Singapore (and other cities around the world), General Assembly provides coding, data, design, and marketing bootcamps focused on entry-level roles. It has an 84% graduation rate and a 96% placement rate for its users (General Assembly 2020). It exists to help bridge the gap between job seekers and companies that need talent with relevant skills. Short courses—typically 3 months full-time or part-time over a longer period to provide flexibility—extend the knowledge and skills acquired during formal education. Trained youth are linked directly to internships or full-time jobs, creating employment opportunities that trainees would not overwise be able to access.

Eskwelabs in the Philippines also gives job seekers—youth in particular—access to jobs in the digital sector. Its range of bootcamp-style courses combines upskilling in data literacy, data analytics, and data science with job matching. The average age of learners is 24 years. Job placement depends on the type of course. For longer courses, job interviews with hiring partners are guaranteed. Students can get their tuition fees refunded if they have not secured a job within 9 months. However, 90% obtain jobs within 3 months of graduation and increase their pay, on average, by 50% over their previous jobs.[43]

[43] Eskwelabs.

Revenue generation by charging employers for the job-matching service can drive the sustainability and growth of commercial models. The review identified various pricing approaches adopted by private job-matching providers. They are based on the principle that employers are prepared to pay for good job matching with youth, as benefits outweigh the costs for finding quality young hires. A typical approach is for the employer to pay the job-matching service when a young person is hired. Models that offer additional human resources services to employers can price accordingly, for example, by charging for bundles of services or subscription packages.

There are various pricing options offered to employers to hire youth via the online jobs portal Glints in Singapore (which also operates in other parts of Southeast Asia). Employers can post jobs and receive candidate applications at no charge. Fees are paid when people are hired. A 90-day replacement guarantee is provided, in which an employer who fired a poorly performing hire is offered a new candidate. In addition to matching, monthly subscription packages are available in which Glints manages all aspects of an organization's workforce development, including payroll, regulatory compliance, talent onboarding and engagement, and workspaces. A special pricing package is available to early-stage start-ups.

The blue-collar jobs platform Apna in India developed its own currency—apnaCoins—to support its charging model. Employers pay a fee to advertise vacancies, although some free postings are offered. Employers buy a small, standard, or large hiring plan, depending on the number of applications that they wish to receive. apnaCoins are returned to the employer's account for future use if the target number of applications is not reached. For an additional cost, Apna can proactively reach out to suitable, registered candidates for employers to consider.

Given the focus on hiring flexible labor on the MyRobin platform in Indonesia, reducing the recruitment time and cost for employers is a key part of the value proposition. As well as sourcing good-fit workers, MyRobin enables candidate tracking, salary payments, and other benefits. The fee charged to employers is calculated as a percentage of the wages of workers hired.

Some commercial job-matching models focus on placing youth into quality jobs. As set out in the previous chapters, effective job matching should not just facilitate entry into any job. It should function as a catalyst for quality labor market transitions for young people—helping secure quality first jobs, progress into better-paying jobs, or provide opportunities for upskilling. Job quality has already been highlighted in some public sector models, such as Singapore's Work-Study Certificate. The review also found various private sector models that specify a level of quality in the employment being secured for youth. A key attribute of quality is the level of wages or salary. The time in a job is also an important signal of stable employment. For marginalized youth, working with employers to understand and to accommodate youth's particular needs can also enhance the quality of their experience at work.

The FunctionUp bootcamp in India was launched in 2021 with a guarantee to secure work for youth and to place them into jobs above a minimum level of income (i.e., Rs500,000 [$6,015] per year). Furthermore, tuition fees for courses in software development are only paid once a job is secured. The repayment arrangement is suspended in instances where the job is lost and then is resumed upon reemployment. Courses are highly competitive; selection is through an exam, an interview, and/or completion of a basic programming course. Typically, 100 trainees are selected out of 25,000 applicants for the 6-week training program.

McKinsey's Generation model in Pakistan and India (and other countries) is centered on the sustainability of job placement. The length of time in a job is important to ensure that employment transitions are sustainable. A key target is out-of-work youth who are offered bootcamp-style learning and job placement. Generation has developed a new metric for cost-effectiveness known as cost per employed day, which measures the cost of a matching program per participant based on the number of days of employment in the 6 months after placement. An intervention that places youth into jobs that are temporary or have low retention rates would not, for instance, score highly.

The model used by virtual school Virtualahan in the Philippines illustrates how specialist employer engagement can generate a deep understanding of trainees before they are placed in employment. Virtualahan specializes in matching youth with disabilities into jobs. It works one-on-one with employers to help ensure that they are aware of and can accommodate the specific needs of their new employees. An enabling work environment and culture will significantly enhance the quality of their experiences.

With government funding, corporate finance can also enable progress and innovation in job matching for youth. Some corporations channel corporate social responsibility (CSR) funds into initiatives that strengthen job-matching support for marginalized young job seekers. This can be done at the local level, with a private business directly funding the initiation of a new model. At the multinational level, a company may set up and fund programs in multiple countries, typically through partnerships. The venture capital market can also play a role in seeding new innovations and then scaling up proven approaches. In particular, social venture capital can bring to market new models that aim to have social impact, such as reaching underserved youth.

The job-matching platform for youth with disabilities, SwarajAbility in India, was fully funded to market by Kotak Mahindra Bank, which provided financing from its CSR Project for Education and Livelihood. The bank partnered with a nonprofit CSR associate organization, Youth4Jobs Foundation, which runs the platform. The bank remains one of the principal partners, and technical partners include the Government of India, ILO, Indian Institute of Technology Hyderabad, National Institute of Mental Health and Neuro-Sciences, and Office of the Principal Scientific Adviser.

Blue-collar workers' platform MyRobin in Indonesia received funding from a social investor, Accion. Its Venture Lab is an early-stage impact investor that promotes financial inclusion. It participated in a pre-Series A round of financing for MyRobin in January 2022. After registering 3 million workers in 270 cities, MyRobin was acquired by an India-based human resources technology solutions company, BetterPlace, in early 2023. The majority stake held by BetterPlace will enable MyRobin to expand into Southeast Asia.

Pathways to Progress II is Citi Foundation's youth economic opportunity CSR initiative. It has provided $275 million to programs in over 80 countries and areas since its inception in 2014. A new 3-year, $100-million commitment in 2020 for Asia and the Pacific was provided to respond to the youth employment challenges precipitated by the COVID-19 pandemic. Funding is channeled to partners with local and technical expertise to deliver on shared priorities. In India, a $10-million commitment aims to deliver demand-driven skills training to 200,000 low-income young people, with an expected job placement rate of at least 70% in India's growth industries.

Private sector interventions help reach untapped markets. Parameter 1 looked at approaches to vulnerability targeting and inclusivity. The private sector also plays a role in serving demographic groups beyond the reach of public job-matching systems by tackling barriers that exclude some youth from some industries and enabling more inclusive hiring. One growth area in the private job-matching market is support for informal workers. Most of the young labor force in developing and emerging markets work informally. In line with the nature of their work, they also tend to seek jobs through informal and hyperlocal channels, such as community and peer-to-peer networks and newspapers. Digital matching models, including for informal workers, are further examined under Parameter 4. Other examples related to improving inclusivity of job-matching models are presented under Parameter 1.

Job-matching app Apna was launched in 2019 in India to tap the job-matching market for blue-collar and low-skilled workers. It has scaled up quickly and now operates in over 70 cities, including many smaller ones. Available via mobile app, it expands economic opportunities for the emerging workforce of frontline workers,[44] gig workers, and contractual staff. Some jobs can be secured within 2 days. The matching algorithm operates at a hyperlocal level.

The bootcamp organizer General Assembly in Singapore primarily targets educated youth but also runs a social impact program that expands access to quality jobs for underrepresented low-income communities. Scholarships for and reductions in course fees are funded through partnerships with employers. Globally, General Assembly provides over 600 scholarships for programs valued at $9 million. Collaboration with nonprofit organizations helps identify and support nontraditional students and introduce relevant program adaptations for them. General Assembly also donates training curricula to organizations that work with hard-to-reach youth and other marginalized communities who cannot access mainstream courses.

Online digital skills school Eskwelabs in the Philippines has a specific outreach initiative to improve access to jobs for at-home mothers. Its Data Literacy Skills Course is delivered over 4 hours and is available only to beneficiaries of Filipina Homebased Moms, a social enterprise. Filipina Homebased Moms is an e-learning platform and community for mothers who wish to upskill so they can work from home. It provides upskilling, job search and matching, and other support, often with other partners.

[44] Frontline workers are those who need to be physically present at worksites to do their jobs (Maroney 2019).

Private sector models can match youth to jobs in growth sectors. More attention is being given to how to grow sectors with potential for creating a high number of quality jobs for youth. Job-matching models are emerging that specialize in placing youth in particular sectors, such as the digital sector. Bootcamps provide an alternative route to employment in various technology fields, while innovative social enterprise approaches help vulnerable groups access digital jobs. The review found that job-matching models for green jobs are only nascent in Asia and the Pacific. One model is featured that caters for youth. A further approach matches youth to jobs in growth sectors identified at the local level.

Digital Divide Data in Cambodia runs an impact sourcing model that enables access to diverse digital careers for underserved youth. It upskills youth to do outsourced digital work for clients or to secure jobs with employers in its partner network. Outsourced services include content digitization, data labeling and annotation for machine learning, and web scraping. Clients span sectors from AgriTech to autonomous driving vehicles and include high-profile businesses and universities. Digital Divide Data also contributes to scholarships and loans for high-potential youth to pursue higher education.

Green Collar Careers in Singapore is a job-matching platform specializing in jobs for the green economy. It hosts a website for jobs available at a network of sustainable companies and curates vacancies from other recruitment sites. Jobs vary by contract type and nature of the work, and youth internship positions are included. Industries include plant-based food, renewable energy, and urban farming. In 2021, 540 jobs were posted, but this fell to less than 20 in 2023.[45]

McKinsey's social impact model Generation helps youth upskill and find jobs in local in-demand sectors with acute skills and human resource demands. Across Generation's global operations, 38 professions are supported in five sectors: customer service and sales, technology, health care, green jobs, and skilled trades (e.g., sewing machine operation). In Pakistan, courses are available for freelance programmers (i.e., digital marketing and graphic design) and junior full stack developers. Upon completion of the training, youth are supported to prepare for job interviews with software companies and start-ups. The job placement rate of Pakistan graduates in the 90 days after program completion is 86%, and 85% of those placed remain employed for at least 1 year.[46]

Finally, the private sector makes an important contribution by developing digital tools that strengthen the job-matching function. Private sector innovations are transforming the job-matching process through the application of advanced technologies such as machine learning and AI. Digital innovations are discussed under Parameter 4.

45 The review further found that other environment job boards in the region—such as the India-based nonprofit ClimateAsia.org—post skilled positions but do not feature filtering for entry-level jobs nor offer upskilling courses. The job board of the media company eco-business.com, headquartered in Singapore, has an "entry-level" tab, but at the time of writing, no opportunities are available.

46 Generation.

Public–Private Collaboration

Network-based models are increasingly common. Many of the models identified in the review feature some sort of collaboration or partnership arrangement. A typical arrangement is a network of partner employers that hire youth, or a range of stakeholders working together to help meet the needs of youth to be job ready and to secure employment. Collaboration brings a range of benefits, including expanding the breadth of services, reaching out to marginalized youth, strengthening connections with employers, and maximizing the efficiency of the job-matching process. Some practices have already been incorporated in the preceding discussion. The following examples spotlight selected practical mechanisms of collaboration and partnership.

The Work-Study Certificate in Singapore illustrates the value of a network of employer partners. Interested firms want to strengthen their entry-level talent pipeline, so the government brokers connections between graduates and employer partners in key industries. Suitable candidates are matched to jobs in their fields of study, then supported through training and mentoring. To ensure that the young graduates build skills relevant to employer priorities and receive career progression support, training development plans are designed by employers for each candidate. Employers also play an advisory role in shaping the program to maintain its relevance to industry needs.

The skills-based job matching and data portal ASEEM in India was created as a multistakeholder model to bridge the supply of—and demand for—skilled labor. It brings together a range of stakeholders—government, employers, agencies and aggregators, training partners, and job seekers. The portal was initiated by the Ministry of Skill Development and Entrepreneurship and integrates different government portals (e.g., skills) and schemes (e.g., migration). The private sector helps design the presentation of data on the portal to maximize attraction for industry. It also collaborates to drive usage. For example, as part of its support for SMEs, a commercial bank can signpost clients to ASEEM to access resources to strengthen hiring capabilities.

Aspen Institute's GOYN is also intentionally a multistakeholder scheme. Once it has identified a potential operating location, a local anchor partner is selected who facilitates effective cross-sector collaboration and coordinates partner commitments. Through collaboration, each model provides joined-up services to promote economic inclusion of marginalized youth, including through employment facilitation. In Pune, India, the anchor partner is Pune City Connect, which specializes in integrated social change strategies through ecosystem collaboration and coordinated action. A participatory design involving youth helps ensure that services are relevant.

Parameter 4: Modalities of Delivery

The review found a range of delivery modalities, which determine the approach of different youth job-matching models. The main variable is the extent to which digital technology is deployed. Issues of service design are closely bound up in the other parameters of targeting (i.e., how best to reach and serve a target group), stakeholders (i.e., infrastructure and capabilities of different types of providers), and service range (i.e., delivery channels that work best for different products and services). In the public sector, progress in e-governance has enabled use of digitized delivery for PES, with a focus on job-matching platforms. The private sector is leading innovation with advanced technologies, such as AI and machine learning, to improve the matching process. This can include, for example, expanding the range of data used to make a match or proactively recommending relevant vacancies to job seekers.

Digital services are changing access to job-matching support. As with other areas of life and work, technology has transformed how people access and experience job matching. Services online and on mobile phones are brought into job seekers' personal environments. They no longer need to move physically to find job-matching support. Digital services directly connect job seekers with employers and, in some cases, training providers and government agencies. Importantly, digital provision is not replacing offline activities. While digital services have transformed job matching, word of mouth via relatives and friends, newspapers, and community job boards continue to be trusted sources of job information. Furthermore, while digitalization provides new opportunities for scale and personalization, it also creates risks, including entrenchment of inequalities through uneven internet access and device ownership, and exploitation—especially of youth—through fraudulent practices such as soliciting fees for fake job interviews.

Work-Net in the Republic of Korea is a leading example of how governments can diversify and expand youth job-matching support by adding digital services to existing on-the-ground employment offices. Young people with internet access have new opportunities to find tailored resources, assess their work readiness, upskill, learn about potential employers, and secure work. Since 2010, an optimized version of Work-Net has been available as a mobile app. The platform has the added benefit of helping youth navigate the proliferation of digital content related to job search by bringing together multiple public and private sites in one place.

Through graduate recruitment site Firstnaukri.com in India, employers no longer must visit campuses to raise their profiles and attract young job seekers. The digital job-matching platform has enhanced graduate recruitment processes for a cohort of youth who are likely to have internet access and smartphones. The shift online has also enabled direct coordination among campuses, employers, and students. Further, Firstnaukri.com extends support to recent graduates who no longer have institutional attachments.

Job-matching platform BDJobs.com in Bangladesh has deployed online and mobile delivery to reach segments of young and informal job seekers who work in roles not usually covered by employment services. The way their services are delivered aligns with offline community habits to ease the digital experience. For example, it is possible to filter advertised jobs on the platform by newspaper. BDJobs.com also provides a range of tools that help users who lack formal work experience develop their profiles and demonstrate suitability for specific roles.

Online platforms function as a connector of a tripartite job-matching ecosystem—youth, employers, and educators and/or trainers. The role of connector across stakeholders is an important value addition of online models. A digital job-matching platform creates the space to connect the stakeholders needed in an enabling support ecosystem for young job seekers and employers. All support services can be made available in one place, and all stakeholders are able to connect and to communicate in an exchange that can lead to better service design and implementation. More governments are adopting a one-stop shop model for youth employment services in recognition of the value of integrating different support types. Specifically, online platforms are being designed or upgraded to break down silos between the different stakeholders in the job-matching and preparation process—training institutions, employers, and youth. In some cases, government agencies are also active on the platforms and can access data or services relevant to public policy.

Jobs and data platform ASEEM in India serves four audiences—skilled candidates; employers, agencies, and aggregators; training partners; and NSDC and government bodies. All services are digitized using advanced technologies, with the portal creating a mechanism to connect across a supply–demand gap in training design and delivery and in youth labor. Alignment across government programs and databases (e.g., mapping migrant labor based on existing schemes) also support stronger policy coherence.

SwarajAbility in India has different entry points for different user groups. The main access is for young job seekers with disabilities. They can register according to their disability type, location, and industry sector. There is a separate navigation system for employers and for institutions (i.e., schools and nongovernment organizations). The cross-sector model connects all types of training providers that cater to the labor market needs of people with disabilities. Academia is also engaged and contributes ongoing research and innovation in digital design and uptake.

The government's jobs and skills platform NISE in Bangladesh creates a space to connect the supply and demand of youth skilling and employment, addressing a key public policy challenge. It brings together public and private trainers and employer stakeholders with youth and facilitates interministerial coordination. Analysis of real-time data generates new insights for policymaking as well as for industry and educational institutions.

There is fast-paced innovation in the mobile market. Mobile apps for job matching is a major growth area. Indeed, the review found that most online portals provide them. In some cases, mobile apps are the only way for youth to access support, even if employers conduct their search and matching with computers. Mobile-based delivery provides convenience, accessibility, inclusivity, and scalability. It is an important field of innovation to reach underserved, low-tech populations, especially informal workers who have a (smart)phone but may not have reliable internet access via computers. Mobile services can also cater to youth with low levels of digital literacy, such as through voice commands or video messaging.

Mobile jobs app Apna was established in India by an ex-Apple executive to tackle the known challenges of delivering job-matching services to labor markets characterized by low levels of trust and high levels of churn. It was designed in collaboration with target users in suburban Mumbai. Its mobile services focus on hyperlocal, informal, part-time, and flexible work, and its capability to match job seekers to jobs within 48 hours is driving uptake. Apna has over 2 million job seekers registered.

MyRobin for blue-collar workers in Indonesia leverages a mobile app to complement social networks for job information sharing and referrals. The app also enables integration of additional services, some of which have not yet been launched. For example, access to formal credit and insurance services may be provided in the future.

SwarajAbility in India opens access to employment opportunities for youth with disabilities. The platform is available through both online and mobile versions to maximize reach. Mobile functionality is key for users with low literacy or digital skills. Its services are provided through a call center as well as SMSs to reach those without smartphones.

Blended service delivery—combining offline and online provision—can help address gaps in coverage and provide comprehensive support. Blending offline and online service provision builds in flexibility for young people's preferences and possibilities. It can also help overcome inequities across job search capacities and infrastructure access. For example, educated youth with time and income may maximize their learning outcomes by attending a full-time, on-campus bootcamp. For lower-income, lower-skilled youth who need to continue to work to make ends meet, other formats for learning are more accessible. Isolated, rural communities can benefit from combined low-tech mobile service access with more intensive, guided support from traveling counselors via local offices.

The National Career Service in India is available via multiple channels to maximize reach and accessibility for different profiles of young job seekers. Online, there is a one-stop shop employment portal through a mobile app. A call center provides support in seven languages toll free. In addition, offline model career centers provide in-person employment services. These centers operate the Young Professionals Scheme, in which one young professional aged 24–40 years is employed at each center for a 2-year period extendable to 5 years. The aim is to "utilize the knowledge, energy and fresh way of thinking of these young social leaders to help better transform the emerging landscape of employment services and career counselling in India."[47]

In Singapore, the government's online jobs and training platform MyCareersFuture links to offline career guidance and job-matching services. Via the platform, users can register to meet with career officers at career centers as part of the Careers Connect scheme.

[47] Government of India, Ministry of Labour and Employment, DGE. Model Career Centre (MCC) and Interlinking of Employment Exchanges.

There are 3 main centers and 20 satellite centers. A traveling service, Careers Connect On-the-Go, brings support closer to communities in designated locations on selected dates. Remote video calls and a text-messaging service for on-demand support are also available.

The JobStart program in the Philippines developed an online portal, Youth Employment Exchange, in response to pandemic-induced service disruptions to the main modality of in-person provision via public employment service offices. It is designed to connect these offices and businesses for information exchange and virtual engagement. Employers can post vacancies for youth, upload required documentation for job placement of youth, register for events, monitor trainees' progress, and apply for subsidies.

Innovations in advanced technologies—notably AI and machine learning—are changing job matching for both job seekers and employers. Automated processes make connections between youth and available work. It is no longer necessary for youth to trawl through unsuitable job openings or for employers to screen unsuitable candidates. Recommended applicants are sent directly to employers, significantly reducing inefficiency, and young job seekers are more likely to stay motivated and engaged in search when matched to appropriate jobs. Automated processes rely on high-quality data, robust scraping and analysis, and algorithms that avoid bias or discrimination. Technologies are also prompting a shift to more skills- and competence-based hiring rather than reliance on formal qualifications (as discussed under Parameter 2).

In 2020, the Republic of Korea's public employment platform Work-Net introduced a new tool called The Work. Through AI and machine learning, it can match registered job seekers with employers based on analyses of job seeker competencies and job specifications. This job-matching technology builds on a prior innovation that passively sent suitable job recommendations daily to job seekers. Development required a regulatory amendment to allow outside data to be included in The Work system.

A proprietary matching algorithm underpins many commercial job portals, and Singapore-based Glints has developed its TalentHunt tool by applying AI and machine learning. Suitable candidates are curated for employers for specific vacancies or as part of an ongoing talent search arrangement, depending on hiring needs. Filtering and evaluation of candidates are data-enabled and conducted on dashboards. The application process is automated and fully managed through the software.

The Government of Singapore has also invested in advanced technologies to support job matching through MyCareersFuture. The system generates a matching score between a job seeker's skills and the skills required in job descriptions as posted by employers. The score is derived by machine learning based on skills keyed in by users and their resumes. This creates a different skills typology from the Singapore Skills Frameworks used by a complementary government scheme called MySkillsFuture.

5

FINDINGS AND RECOMMENDATIONS

This review of youth job-matching models has analyzed key practices, features, and innovations in Asia and the Pacific. The main findings are presented in this section, drawn from the review of models and previous chapters that set out the importance of youth as a life stage that involves multiple transitions, including transitions into, back into, and within the labor market. These chapters also situated the job-matching function in the wider youth employment support system. Accordingly, the findings incorporate broader insights about the employment facilitation ecosystems in the region. Examples from outside of the region are cited, where appropriate, so that Asia and the Pacific can learn from good practices elsewhere.

Each finding presented in this section is followed by a recommendation. In many cases, the recommendations encourage stakeholders to adopt the effective and innovative approaches contained in the models reviewed. In others, they build on broader insights about the strengths and weaknesses of various job facilitation ecosystems. Innovative practices found outside of the region are also shared to illustrate opportunities for better practice. In all cases, recommendations are meant as constructive encouragement to stakeholders to improve the matching of young job seekers not just into any job—but into a quality job. This report recommends effective job matching as an intervention to support better employment transitions for youth.

5.1 Building an Understanding of Youth Transitions

Young job seekers experience several parallel life-cycle transitions as they attempt to enter the world of work. They face a host of personal, social, and role-in-society changes and growth experiences that affect their ability to secure and to retain employment. Youth is a formative time of life as well as an important stage in the life course. Experiences during that time determine future employment and career development.

> **RECOMMENDATION 1** Policymakers and other stakeholders are encouraged to understand the full set of transitions that youth are making. Stakeholders can adopt a "youth transitions" mindset as the foundation of thinking about support for youth. This mindset will help them design better programs that enable youth to make fluid and progressive employment transitions into quality jobs.

Youth (employment) transitions are often not linear. Young people may secure work but then lose employment and be bounced out of the labor market. They may need support to regain confidence and work and to build resilience to navigate labor market transitions. They may move from school to work but also from work back into education and training. They may juggle different forms of work (e.g., part-time, contract, gig, or entrepreneurial) with attempts to upskill and to gain experience. Their early years thus may represent a zigzagging path into and around employment—not a linear one.

> **RECOMMENDATION 2** Youth support planners should recognize that many young people do not follow a simple, one-off, school-to-work transition. Youth need different types of support depending on their current engagement with the labor market and to support nonlinear future transitions.

Job matching makes a central contribution to inclusive labor markets for youth. Concerted investment can be made to strengthen the connection between young people who need work and employers that lack talent with appropriate skills. Well-designed job-matching interventions take a long-term perspective; they do not only create a one-off transaction (i.e., a single job match) between job seeker and employer. They can help smooth the bumpy transitions that young people navigate through the labor market. Targeted interventions can help open access to quality jobs for young people who would typically be excluded, for example, due to gender-based constraints or discrimination. Job matching is particularly needed when labor markets have been disrupted during times of socioeconomic upheaval.

> **RECOMMENDATION 3** Job matching should be emphasized as part of policy and program packages for youth. Intermediation support anchored in job matching can be combined with supply-side (employability) and demand-side (quality job creation) interventions. Providing job matching alongside skills training programs can help improve young people's labor market attachment.

Securing work for young people is good; placing them into quality jobs is better. In much of Asia and the Pacific, most of the work is informal, including for young people. This means that working conditions are poor, wages are low, hours are long and unpredictable, breaks are short, job-related social security is nonexistent, and satisfaction is limited. A key challenge is to improve the quality of work for youth, as a good start in the labor market sets a course toward better future outcomes.

> **RECOMMENDATION 4** Effective job matching should seek to move school graduates directly into good, formal sector jobs or help pull working youth out of the informal labor market and into formal or better-quality conditions. Close collaboration with employers to hire, prepare, retain, and support young workers is an important feature of facilitation into quality jobs, including through practices such as minimum earning thresholds and post-placement support. The availability of quality work is a prerequisite.

Overall, four parameters can define and differentiate job-matching programs, based on the concept of "3W1H." The first "W" is "who." This is about targeting and whether the program is exclusive to youth or merely includes them as well as what subgroups within youth are targeted (e.g., those with disabilities or blue-collar workers). The second "W" is "what"—the type of service or services offered and if matching is complemented with job preparation, search, or other support. The third "W" focuses on "which" types of stakeholders are involved—public, private, or nonprofit organizations. Finally, the one "H" is "how" the mechanisms are delivered and includes whether the service is provided through the internet, in-person, or both.

RECOMMENDATION 5 Governments and other stakeholders can benefit from recognizing that youth are best served by support tailored to their specific needs. There are a variety of players catering to different youth segments, providing different services, and using different methods to involve them in the labor market. This recognition can be useful in avoiding duplication in programs, enabling innovation by the private sector, and in identifying gaps in provision that are leaving some youth cohorts underserved.

5.2 Designing Job Matching to Underpin Positive Youth Employment Transitions

Combining job matching with other support services helps cater to the complexity of youth transitions. First, this means linking job matching to other types of intermediation support, mainly job search and job preparation. Second, job matching and any other intermediation services can be part of a wider, holistic support package for youth. Multicomponent approaches are particularly common for disadvantaged youth, as they help address multiple, interconnected needs. This integrated approach to youth employment support means job matching needs to be part of a well-coordinated policy ecosystem.

RECOMMENDATION 6 At the policy and program levels, designers and implementers should consider where job matching fits in the wider support ecosystem for youth. To provide easy-to-access and coordinated services to youth, linking matching to preexisting skills-based support may be relevant. Often partnerships, networks, or other collaboration models provide efficient mechanisms for stakeholders to combine services.

Program design and implementation can improve job quality and transition prospects. The review identified different ways in which youth job-matching models aim to help young job seekers secure quality jobs and manage future moves. Some of these incorporate linkages to complementary services, including improving workplace conditions and retention rates (e.g., through providing post-match support; securing higher starting salaries or formal roles to begin a positive upward cycle; and providing job preparation support, like skills training and labor market knowledge to enhance future pathways). Table 3 contains examples, given this report's focus on a transitions approach to youth job matching. Ten different design and delivery adaptations were identified.

RECOMMENDATION 7 Programs to support youth job matching should avoid treating matching as a one-off transaction. Instead, they should incorporate complementary features that increase the likelihood of a good, long-term match between youth and employers and support youth to continue to chart fulfilling and productive learning-earning pathways.

Table 3: 10 Practices to Improve Job Matching for Job Quality and Effective Transitions

1. Secure formal wage employment • Work-Study Certificate, Singapore • Build a network of partner employers to provide formal wage work for young graduates	**6. Link complementary services** • MyRobin, Indonesia • Provide financial services alongside job matching to improve financial inclusion and earning capability of informal workers
2. Earn a minimum level of income • FunctionUp, India • Place youth into jobs with firms that agree to pay them an agreed minimum level of income	**7. Prepare employers** • Virtualahan, Philippines • Provide services to employers to be better prepared to hire and to work with youth with disabilities, and improve their workplace experiences
3. Address skills gaps • BDjobs.com, Bangladesh • Offer digital assessment tools and training alongside job matching for youth to identify skills gaps and then re-/upskill	**8. Measure sustainability of job matches** • Generation, Pakistan • Measure how long youth stay in work compared to program costs, and build awareness of achieving long-term employment outcomes
4. Build job market capabilities • Apna, India • Combine social networks with job-matching services to build social capital and skilling courses to improve employability	**9. Build networks of employer partners** • Digital Divide Data, Cambodia • Open up access to quality jobs in high-profile companies in the digital sector out of reach of disadvantaged target youth
5. Provide post-placement support • Deen Dayal Upadhyaya Grameen Kaushalya Yojana (DDU-GKY), India • Give financial stipends to help poor, rural youth settle and stay in new jobs	**10. Connect the ecosystem** • National Intelligence for Skills, Education, Employment and Entrepreneurship (NISE), Bangladesh • Match youth and firms hiring in in-demand sectors, and provide advanced industry analytics and labor market information for training development and policymaking

Source: Authors.

The ways that youth job-matching models are financed can improve access to quality jobs. Public services tend to be offered free of charge. Private sites normally do not charge a fee for a job seeker to post a curriculum vitae or to apply for a job, or for an employer to post vacancies. Instead, fees are normally charged to employers after matches are made and young job seekers are hired. There are also innovative financing approaches to preparatory courses for skilling and digital bootcamps, in which tuition fees for training are only paid if jobs are secured. The social finance sector may be a source to seed and to scale innovative approaches, especially those targeting job seekers left behind. This is driving innovation and upscaling in the mobile-based job-matching market.

RECOMMENDATION 8 Paying after matches are made and jobs are secured creates a strong incentive for job-matching (and training) programs to be effective. Further use of incentive mechanisms should be explored for publicly provided matching services. The social finance sector can also be encouraged to invest in job-matching solutions, especially for disadvantaged youth.

Digital technology is a major driver of innovation in services and expansion in access. The ways in which services are delivered can affect the accessibility, relevance, and effectiveness of support for youth. Services are provided in-person and digitally—and the two modalities are increasingly being blended for scale and inclusion. There has been a rise in the use of mobile apps, which help provide simplified access and services to youth, including to young informal workers. A segment of the digital market is growing to expand access to quality digital jobs for underserved youth.

> **RECOMMENDATION 9** To maximize inclusion, stakeholders should balance and blend in-person and technology-based support to young job seekers. Provision should respond to the varying levels of digital access among different cohorts of youth as well as to behavioral preferences regarding uses of technologies (i.e., high mobile usage among lower-income groups).

Machine learning and AI are improving job matching. Rapid innovation in these techniques is improving the speed and relevance of matching job seekers and employers. These techniques make full use of data contained in vacancy postings and job seeker files. Less time spent on unproductive searches builds job seeker confidence and allows employers to focus on talent development. Digital approaches to hiring, including algorithm-based methods, can enhance objectivity and transparency—but there is a risk that they may also reinforce some biases and discrimination. Advanced digital techniques are being adopted by many youth job-matching services, both public and private. Their use also extends to other parts of the matching process. For example, the AI-powered profiling tool adopted by Estonia's PES accurately segments job seekers into different service streams by their probability of rapidly integrating or reintegrating into the labor market.[48] It does so by assessing youth's main factors for entering employment and returning into unemployment (OECD 2022c).

> **RECOMMENDATION 10** Knowledge exchange and public–private collaboration can be nurtured to accelerate the uptake of advanced technologies in improving job matching for youth while strengthening the regulatory environment to ensure fair and inclusive hiring practices. In particular, PES can be supported in applying machine learning and AI to youth job matching, including in lower-income countries.

5.3 Building a Coherent and Coordinated Support Ecosystem for Youth Job Matching

The diversity and range of youth job-matching services is growing in Asia and the Pacific. This growth is part of an effort to meet the needs of different cohorts of young job seekers, who often face multiple barriers to securing quality jobs. It also serves a rising demand from employers for more effective ways to recruit job-ready youth with relevant skills and workplace competences. From the job seeker perspective, a key focus of programs is smoothing first transitions into work, but some programs focus on reactivating left-behind youth who are unemployed or have dropped out of the labor market.

48 The accuracy rate is 95%.

A range of specialist providers now support specific cohorts of disadvantaged youth in some countries and areas. A particular focus group identified in the review is young people with disabilities; a particular sector focus is developing pathways for disadvantaged youth into digital work. For employers, job matching is being integrated with other human resources support services that help them in all areas of recruiting and retaining talent.

The review identified six categories of youth job-matching models: (i) government online platforms, (ii) targeted government programs, (iii) commercial digital platforms (for-profit), (iv) targeted social impact models, (v) digital bootcamps, and (vi) multistakeholder partnerships (corporate-funded).

> **RECOMMENDATION 11** More rigorous evaluation is needed of which job-matching models are the most effective, including which work best for different cohorts of youth. The findings can be used to refine existing models and to create new ones. The focus should be not only on the effectiveness for job seekers but also on learning which services and delivery modalities best meet the hiring needs of employers.

Among subregions, Southeast Asia has the most youth job-matching models selected for the review. In particular, there is growth in commercial and social digital ventures in this subregion. Further, 7 out of 13 countries in Southeast Asia are represented. Singapore has built flagship digital job-matching services that are generating lessons for others. The Republic of Korea is also a pioneer in this field, although administrative capacity in both countries limits replicability to less-developed economies. Good practices can also be found across other subregions. Models in the large, populous country of India demonstrate services delivery at different administrative levels and how to rationalize services (i.e., reorganize them to improve efficiency). Indeed, 9 of the 31 models are from India. In Central and West Asia, there is limited private-led innovation; instead, governments are strengthening employment services, including linkages with employers. Limited activity was identified in the Pacific, where informal employment practices are prevalent, and formal employment services are not yet advanced.

> **RECOMMENDATION 12** Countries and areas can review practices from other subregions and assess opportunities for strengthened or new support for youth job matching. Ideas for serving particular labor market dynamics, such as informality or youth cohorts like young people with disabilities, can be assessed for applicability to a specific context. While there is considerable diversity and range when considering the region as a whole, few countries and areas provide the full complement of services reaching all youth segments.

Meeting the demand in youth job matching requires a range of stakeholders. Governments play a key role in ensuring the scalability of provision and in delivering support for marginalized youth, such as those in rural areas. Governments are also acting increasingly as aggregators of job matching and other employment support for youth, including through digital platforms. Social entrepreneurship and nonprofit initiatives are also important in helping reach underserved youth, while a vibrant start-up scene of private sector job-matching platforms is innovating and expanding service offerings for young job seekers. Some models specialize in specific industry sectors, especially high-growth sectors, such as digital technology or, to a much lesser extent, the green economy.

The provision of services by for-profit companies is part of a wider expansion of internet-based, digital-matching services, also known as job portals, job (web)sites, or job vacancy sites. Some services were initiated and funded by international development partners working with governments.

> **RECOMMENDATION 13** Governments can view the diversification of providers as a positive development, while being vigilant in identifying continued gaps in services provision. As well, governments may seek to assess whether they should scale back services, reposition themselves, or convene partnerships if private providers are servicing the main youth job market. International and domestic development partners can play a part in enabling policy reform, piloting and scaling services for underserved youth, and convening knowledge exchange to expand support.

5.4 Gaps in the Youth Job-Matching Landscape in Asia and the Pacific

The provision of youth job-matching support can fragment across government ministries and agencies. Job-matching services can be offered simultaneously by ministries of labor, education (and skills), and rural development and related agencies. This can create policy incoherence in a government's youth employment efforts and stoke confusion and uncertainty about access for young job seekers looking for support. If programs by different ministries use discordant metrics for certification and credentialing of skills, this can add to the problem. There are, however, some good examples in and outside of the region of governments adopting more coordinated policy and program approaches. The Government of Australia, for instance, undertook wide institutional and policy reform in which youth affairs was reintroduced under the Department of Education, Skills and Employment; a new crosscutting youth policy framework is being built by listening and responding to young people's needs. Also, Finland has a one-stop shop, featuring a multisector partnership that simplifies access for youth to job support programs (ILO 2020b).

> **RECOMMENDATION 14** Governments are encouraged to provide a joined-up approach to youth employment policy that addresses the interconnected needs and aspirations of young people. These can span wider personal, social, and cultural domains, such as mental health or family permission for young women to travel to work. Policy coherence requires institutional and budgetary leadership and coordination by one or more ministries and agencies. Joined-up approaches are further strengthened through collaboration with the private and nonprofit sectors.

There are limited public–private partnerships at scale in the region for youth job matching. Several high-income—and even middle-income—countries have comprehensive, blended (i.e., online and offline) youth job-matching support systems. However, none feature a major private partner. Experience from outside of the region shows that this can become a highly effective model for supporting the transitions of youth into sustainable employment, reaching not only at-risk young people but also employers that would not traditionally engage in government job schemes or with hard-to-reach youth. Harambee and the SA Youth model in South Africa provides a useful example (Box 8).

Box 8

Harambee—South Africa's Transitions Approach to Job Matching

Harambee is a nonprofit youth employment accelerator in South Africa that was founded in 2011. It works in partnership with the government to place youth from disadvantaged households in hard-to-reach communities into entry-level jobs with a range of employers. Its job-matching model has evolved based on learning what is needed to keep youth in work for at least 1 year (i.e., pathway management). Sequenced support helps identify and profile youth and bridge them into job readiness through integrated support centered on behavioral interventions. The training includes a component on "how to keep your job and turn it into a career." Another component trains youth on how to work in unstructured and minimally supervised environments, such as small and medium-sized enterprises.

Working on both the supply and demand sides of the job-matching equation, specialist assistance is also provided to employers (e.g., job profiling) to strengthen their recruitment reach and effectiveness, with tailored solutions for small businesses. Harambee also invests in leading digital technologies to scale through big data analytics and machine-learning algorithms. These include geolocation techniques to account for informal settlements and commutes, predictive behavioral metrics, and feature-phone mobile services (i.e., not smartphones) to reach underserved populations.

Harambee is a lead partner in a national platform, SA Youth, which serves to aggregate opportunities and link unemployed young people to jobs and work experiences. SA Youth was launched in 2021 as part of the Presidential Youth Employment Intervention. It brings together eight government departments led by the Department of Employment and Labour with a network of other stakeholders under a coordinated national plan of action that aims to "contribute towards a South Africa where youth are actively participating in the economy with greater dignity and a sense of agency over their contribution to society."

Over its first decade of operation, Harambee reached over 1 million youth and worked with more than 500 employer partners. The next 5-year plan aims to triple their impact.

Sources: Altbeker (2015), Harambee (2021), and Google Cloud. Harambee Youth Employment Accelerator: Solving the Youth Unemployment Challenge.

RECOMMENDATION 15 To scale the reach of services and to strengthen policy coherence, governments can consider building broad-based public–private partnership models. In particular, these can help improve outreach to hard-to-reach young job seekers and employers. It can also help reduce fragmentation across disparate service offerings. High-level government leadership and a high-performing lead nongovernment partner are important features.

Some countries and areas still do not cater to youth job matching in public employment services. In Asia and the Pacific, there are some promising tendencies among governments to invest in strengthening PES, youth targeting, and job matching. The Republic of Korea and Singapore are both on the cutting edge of blended services provision for youth (and adults). Bangladesh is pioneering experimental ways to use data to advance better provision. Yet, in some countries and areas, there is a lack of youth-focused programs, in some cases, as part of a broader lack of employment services.

Weak institutional capacity often holds back progress. PES may provide vocational training, skills certification, and employment placement, yet a lack of resources and data—and limited information sharing and engagement with job seekers and employers—limit the uptake and value of these tools.

> **RECOMMENDATION 16** It is important for governments to build the capabilities of PES so that they can play their part in catering to the needs of young job seekers. Given preferences to find work through alternative channels, especially private providers and informal networks, PES should streamline and focus their support to address gaps, depending on the state of other job-matching provision. Aggregation of services and data can be an important contribution by governments to simplify access for inexperienced youth and to strengthen the capabilities of other stakeholders.

Job-matching services for green jobs is nascent but has potential. As a niche market, there are few dedicated green job-matching services in the region. The only model identified in the review did not provide complementary services and posted only a small number of jobs. Standards to classify environment-related job positions, including in nonenvironment industry companies, need to be further defined as the market for green jobs grows. The green economy is growing as a source of wage work as well as self-employment for youth.

> **RECOMMENDATION 17** For now, green jobs will continue to be advertised primarily along with jobs in other sectors. If there is adequate demand to fill green job vacancies for youth, however, the private sector may provide dedicated services. Targeted programs to prepare youth and to connect them into quality green jobs will help accelerate the take-up of opportunities in the green economy.

Young people in rural areas are generally not well served by job-matching services. Only two targeted programs were identified for the review, although another featured migration services for rural communities, and some PES, do operate satellite or traveling services. Rural-based job seekers often face spatial constraints to accessing quality work, including lack of digital and transport infrastructure and labor market information. Moreover, there may be few formal job opportunities in rural areas. There, the search by employers for staff and by youth for jobs continues to rely on informal matching processes, although the use of digital sites has opened access to job matching for job seekers—for those with digital access. Still, most of the jobs posted are available in urban areas.

> **RECOMMENDATION 18** Rural youth should be aided in connecting to job opportunities elsewhere (i.e., in urban or peri-urban areas). Efforts should also be made to increase the quantity and quality of work available in their home communities and to match youth to those opportunities. Expanding access of rural youth to digital job-matching services through mobile phones and to offline support through satellite or mobile-traveling PES should be encouraged.

6 CONCLUSION

This review of youth job-matching models in Asia and the Pacific comes to two very broad conclusions. The first is encouraging; the second poses a challenge. **The first conclusion is that stakeholders have recognized the specific needs of young job seekers and put into place job-matching services tailored to those needs.** This is foundational because it removes doubt about whether youth should be treated differently than adults. It demonstrates that governments and other stakeholders have acted, designing specific services for young people. **The second conclusion is that while the range of models is encouraging, their coverage is insufficient to address the region's significant youth employment challenge.** There is high potential to incorporate job matching into more youth programs and to upscale the promising practices and features identified in this report to enable better labor market transitions.

The report also comes to several more specific conclusions. These are woven into the report and synthesized in the previous chapter. Five are highlighted here.

First, "youth" is a period of multiple transitions that includes employment transitions but also personal transitions that affect young people's engagement with work and the job market. Some transitions can take place simultaneously, and while the initial school-to-work transition is very important, there are many subsequent transitions that are equally crucial (e.g., out of work, back to training, between jobs, or on a path to a quality job). These journeys are better described as a zigzag rather than a straight line.

Second, the goal of job matching is not to place young people into any job but to guide them along a pathway to a quality job. The review identified specific design and implementation practices that can improve how matching supports quality transitions. **Third, job matching can be provided as a single, one-off service, but it is increasingly part of a broader suite of services that may be joined up.** These include other intermediation services, such as assistance with the job search, advice on preparing applications, guidance for interviews, help with building online profiles, and other services to increase employability (e.g., short-course skills training). Integrating matching with other types of support is more likely to address the multiple needs of youth. Further, sequencing and tailoring the various types of support can help personalize provision.

Fourth, digitalization has been a game changer. To job advertisements in newspapers and noticeboards at public employment offices (where they exist), computer screens and mobile phones have been added as key tools of job search and matching. Personal networks and contacts will continue to be important, but digital now is key, especially for young people who have grown up in the digital era. However, problems of exclusion remain for those without digital access. **Fifth, governments' initial dominance of job-matching services has given way to a more diverse set of providers.** This has been driven by the increase in commercial job sites and bootcamps, meeting demand from both young job seekers and employers as well as the interest of nonprofit and social enterprises in supporting the transitions of young people, especially vulnerable youth.

Finally, it may be useful to state what this report cannot conclude. This has been a mapping exercise; an attempt to see what is out there, underpinned by a conceptual framework that ensures youth job matching is analyzed in terms of youth transitions and the wider youth employment facilitation ecosystem. However, the report does not provide an evaluation of the effectiveness of the 31 models that were selected, nor does it analyze the dynamic evolution of the job-matching market over time as some models persisted and others were discontinued. It assesses what the models do based on four parameters derived from the review—not how well they function or have evolved. There are very few studies available based on rigorous evaluations—there should be more.

APPENDIX 1

ONLINE RESOURCES FOR SELECTED JOB-MATCHING MODELS

CATEGORY A: GOVERNMENT ONLINE PORTALS	
Work-Net, Korea	Government of the Republic of Korea, Ministry of Employment and Labor.
	Government of the Republic of Korea, Ministry of the Interior and Safety. Work-Net (Employment Information Platform).
	Kring, S. and S. Elder. 2022. *Digital Solutions and Formalization: E-Formalization Case Study on the Republic of Korea*. Geneva: ILO.
	Observatory of Public Sector Innovation. "The Work", AI Job Recommendation Service Using the National Job Information Platform.
	Korea Employment Information Service. The Best National Employment Information Service.
MyCareersFuture, Singapore	MyCareersFuture.
	SkillsFuture.
	Workforce Singapore. Visit Career Centres.
	Teng, R. 2022. User Experience Is Central to Successful Job Matching, Says Director of Singapore's MyCareersFuture Portal. GovInsider. 30 August.
National Intelligence for Skills, Education, Employment and Entrepreneurship (NISE), Bangladesh	Government of Bangladesh. National Intelligence for Skills, Education, Employment and Entrepreneurship (NISE).
	United Nations Development Programme (UNDP). National Intelligence for Skills, Education, Employment & Entrepreneurship (NISE).
National Career Service, India	*The Economic Times*. 2021. India Committed to Improving Employment Outcomes for Youth: Santosh Gangwar. 17 June.
	Government of India, Ministry of Labour and Employment. National Career Service.
	Government of India, Ministry of Labour and Employment. Young Professional Recruitment. National Career Service.
ASEEM, India	ASEEM. Candidate/Jobseeker Interface.
	ASEEM. Employer/Industry Interface.
	Government of India, Ministry of Skill Development and Entrepreneurship. 2021. Aatmanirbhar Skilled Employee-Employer Mapping (ASEEM) Portal. News release. 6 December.
	Government of India, Ministry of Electronics and Information Technology. Aatamanirbhar Skilled Employee Employer Mapping (ASEEM) Portal. Vikaspedia.
	HDFC Bank. Everything to Know about Aatmanirbhar Skilled Employee-Employer Mapping (ASEEM).
	National Skill Development Corporation. ASEEM, a Skill Management Information System.
	The Times of India. 2020. Government Launches ASEEM Website to Help Workers Get Jobs Online in Their Hometown. 10 July.

continued on next page

Continued

CATEGORY B: TARGETED GOVERNMENT PROGRAMS	
Work-Study Certificate, Singapore	MySkillsFuture. SkillsFuture Work-Study Programmes. SkillsFuture Work-Study Certificate. Temasek Polytechnic. For Individuals.
Deen Dayal Upadhyaya Grameen Kaushalya Yojana (DDU-GKY), India	Government of India, Ministry of Rural Development. Deen Dayal Upadhyaya Grameen Kaushalya Yojana.
JobStart, Philippines	Asian Development Bank (ADB). 2018. Social Protection Brief: Reducing Youth Not in Employment, Education, or Training through JobStart Philippines. *ADB Briefs*. No. 87. Manila. ADB. n.d. *JobStart Philippines Program Overview*. Manila. Camero, J. S. 2016. JobStart Philippines Program Now Republic Act 10869. News release. Government of the Philippines, House of Representatives. 2 July. Government of the Philippines, Department of Labor and Employment. JobStart Philippines Program. JobStart. JobStart Philippines Program. JobStart. JobStart Philippines 2022–2027 National Rollout Strategy.
Pradhan Mantri Kaushal Vikas Yojana (PMKVY) 3.0, India	*The Economic Times*. 2019. NSDC, KnackApp Join Hands to Counsel Youth for Career Guidance. 22 July. KnackApp. National Skill Development Corporation. 2020. Monthly Dashboard. October. Pradhan Mantri Kaushal Vikas Yojana.
Skills and Employability Enhancement Project, Tajikistan	ADB. 2020. ADB's $30 Million Grant to Support Labor Migrants, Youth, and Women in Tajikistan. News release. 1 July. ADB. 2020. *Report and Recommendation of the President to the Board of Directors: Proposed Loan to Tajikistan for the Skills and Employability Enhancement Project*. Manila. ADB. 2020. *Gender Action Plan: Skills and Employability Enhancement Project*. Manila. Asia-Plus. 2021. ADB Awards a US$30 Million Grant to Tajikistan to Support Enhancing Skills and Employability. 20 January.
Urban Youth Employment Project II, Papua New Guinea	World Bank. Urban Youth Employment Project II. Projects and Operations. World Bank. 2020. Project Appraisal Document on a Proposed Credit in the Amount of SDR25.5 Million (US$35 Million Equivalent) to the Independent State of Papua New Guinea for an Urban Youth Employment Project II. Washington, DC.

continued on next page

Continued

CATEGORY C: COMMERCIAL DIGITAL JOB PLATFORMS	
JobsCentral BrightMinds, Singapore	BrightMinds. CareerBuilder. CareerBuilder. An Introduction to SocialReferral. CareerBuilder. BrightMinds. Careers Content. 2019. *Job Search Avenues.* Singapore. JobsCentral Learning.
Glints, Singapore	Glints. Glints Academy. Glints Expert Class. Glints for Employers. Monk's Hill Ventures. 2021. *The Southeast Asia Tech Talent Compensation Report.* Singapore. Mulia, K. 2020. Why Recruitment Startup Glints Is Focusing on Education. TechinAsia. 30 March. Singapore Economic Development Board. Glints.
JobHopin, Viet Nam	JobHopin. Panday, S. 2020. These Are the Hottest Positions in Ho Chi Minh City, Da Nang, and Hanoi Right Now: Q&A with JobHopin CEO Kevin Tung Nguyen. KrAsia. 18 June. Shu, C. 2020. JobHopin, a Startup That Wants to Make Job Hunting in Southeast Asia Easier, Raises $2.45 Million Series A. TechCrunch. 11 May.
BDJobs.com, Bangladesh	Abdul Latif Jameel Poverty Action Lab (J-PAL). ADB. 2020. COVID-19 Impact on Job Postings: Real-Time Assessment Using Bangladesh and Sri Lanka Online Job Portals. *ADB Briefs*. No. 135. Manila. BDJobs.com. Future Startup. 2018. Future of Bdjobs.com, Ajkerdeal's Mobile-First Strategy, Entrepreneurship, and Life: An Interview with Fahim Mashroor, Founder and CEO, Bdjobs and Ajkerdeal. 12 April.
Green Collar Jobs, Singapore	GreenCollar. Li, B. L. 2020. Asia's Aspiring 'Green-Collar' Workers Hope for Jobs in COVID Recovery. Reuters. 28 October. *The Straits Times.* 2010. 'Green Collar' Jobs in Singapore: 8,000 and Rising. 10 October. *The Straits Times.* 2020. Covid-19 Heroes: Job Portal for 'Green-Collar' Workers. 23 August.
MyRobin, Indonesia	Accion. 2022. MyRobin.ID, Workforce-as-a-Service Marketplace, Announces Close of Pre-Series A Led by Accion Venture Lab and SOSV. News release. 18 January. *The Hindu Business Line.* 2023. BetterPlace Forays into South-East Asia with Acquisition of Indonesia's MyRobin. 7 February. Limcaoco, P. 2022. Improving the Lives of Blue-Collar Workers in Indonesia through a Digital Platform. Accion. 18 January. MyRobin. Mulia, K. 2021. MyRobin Provides Blue-Collar Workers in Indonesia with Fair Access to Jobs. KrAsia. 29 December. Puri, N. 2021. The Blue-Collar Tech Gold Rush Is Here. TechinAsia. 1 November.

continued on next page

Continued

Apna, India	Anand, S. 2022. Success Story of Apna App: How Apna Became the Fastest Unicorn of India. StartupTalky. 25 May. Apna. Balachandran, M. 2021. How Apna Became One of India's Fastest Unicorns with Almost Zero Annual Revenue. Forbes India. 16 September. Google Cloud. Apna: Optimizing Upskilling and Job Opportunities for Millions across India with Vertex AI. Rai, S. 2021. Blue-Collar Worker App Becomes a Unicorn in Under Two Years. Bloomberg. 15 September. Singh, M. 2021. Tiger Global-Led $100M Investment Makes Apna India's Fastest Unicorn. TechCrunch. 15 September.
CATEGORY D: TARGETED SOCIAL IMPACT MODELS	
Generation, Pakistan/India	Generation: You Employed. Generation: You Employed. Join Us. Generation: You Employed. 2021. *Annual Report 2021: Moving Forward.* PR Newswire. 2021. Generation Tackles Global Unemployment with BlackRock, McKinsey & Company, Microsoft Corp. and Verizon. 11 February.
Digital Divide Data, Cambodia	Digital Divide Data. Romero, J. M., J. Hockenstein, and H. Sahatqija. 2018. Impact Sourcing and Young Social Entrepreneurs: Two Approaches to Tackle Youth Unemployment. World Bank Blogs. 27 November. Singh, S. and Z. Liu. 2020. *S4YE'S Impact Portfolio and Factbook.* Washington, DC: World Bank.
Virtualahan, Philippines	Eskelund, K. R. Heeks, and B. Nicholson. 2019. Exploring an Impact Sourcing Initiative for a Community of People with Disabilities: A Capability Analysis. Paper prepared for the 15th International Conference on Social Implications of Computers in Developing Countries. Dar es Salaam. 1–3 May. Forbes. Ryan Gersava. Virtualahan.
SwarajAbility, India	Arora, S. 2022. Swarajability: India's First AI-Based Job Platform for Persons with Disabilities. Adda24/7. 7 February. SwarajAbility. Youth4Jobs.
Enablecode, Viet Nam	Enablecode. Singh, S. and Z. Liu. 2020. *S4YE'S Impact Portfolio and Factbook.* Washington, DC: World Bank.

continued on next page

Continued

CATEGORY E: DIGITAL BOOTCAMPS	
General Assembly, Singapore	General Assembly. General Assembly. 2021. *General Assembly Student Outcomes Report: 2019.* Singapore. General Assembly. 2022. *General Assembly Student Outcomes Report: 2020.* Singapore. International Telecommunication Union. 2016. *Coding Bootcamps: A Strategy for Youth Employment.* Geneva.
Hacktiv8, Indonesia	Google for Startups. Class of 2020. Hacktiv8. International Bank for Reconstruction and Development and World Bank. 2018. Women Wavemakers: Practical Strategies for Recruiting and Retaining Women in Coding Bootcamps. Washington, DC.
Eskwelabs, Philippines	Bukas. Eskwelabs. Forbes. Eskwelabs.
FunctionUp, India	FunctionUp. Marketing in Asia. 2022. Get Upskilled Now and Pay Later: How FunctionUp Is Kickstarting Careers. 29 July. Mundhra, L. 2022. 30 Startups to Watch: The Startups That Caught Our Eye in May 2022. Inc42. 2 June. National Skill Development Corporation. Our Partners.
CATEGORY F: MULTINATIONAL CORPORATION-LED INITIATIVES	
Young FutureMakers, Thailand	International Labour Organization (ILO). 2021. Young Futuremakers Thailand—Promoting Youth Employability. Bangkok: ILO Country Office for Thailand, Cambodia and Lao People's Democratic Republic. April. Standard Chartered. Futuremakers. United Nations Global Marketplace. 2022. Young Futuremakers Malaysia: Call for Proposals: National Consultancy on Situation Analysis on Youth Employment in Malaysia.
REACH and Future Skills, Viet Nam	Credit Suisse. REACH Vietnam. REACH. Trifigura Foundation. REACH, Vietnam.
Pathways to Progress II, India and Bangladesh	Citi. 2020. Citi and Citi Foundation Expand Global Job Skills-Building Initiative to Improve Employability and Economic Opportunity for Underserved Communities. News release. 17 September. Citi. 2020. Citibank, N.A. *Bangladesh CSR Newsletter 2020.* Dhaka. Citi Foundation. *Dhaka Tribune.* 2019. 400 Underprivileged Women Complete Citi-UCEP Technical Program. 23 June.
Global Opportunities Youth Network, India	Accenture. 2021. Accenture, Global Opportunity Youth Network and SA Youth Join Forces to Reduce Youth Unemployment by 10% in the Next 10 Years. News release. 2 June. The Aspen Institute Forum for Community Solutions. Global Opportunity Youth Network. Global Opportunity Youth Network. Pune City Connect Development Foundation. Pune City Connect.

Source: Authors.

APPENDIX 2

SUMMARY OF DATA OF SELECTED YOUTH JOB-MATCHING MODELS

Table A2.1: Selected Models by Category

	Type	#
A	Government Online Portal	5
B	Targeted Government Program	5
C	Commercial Digital Platform	8
D	Targeted Social Impact Model	5
E	Digital Bootcamp	4
F	Corporate-Funded Multistakeholder Partnership	4
TOTAL		**31**

Source: Authors.

Table A2.2: Country and Area Coverage of Models

Subregion	Country	#
East Asia	Republic of Korea	1
Southeast Asia	Cambodia	1
	Indonesia	2
	Malaysia	1
	Philippines	3
	Singapore	6
	Thailand	1
	Viet Nam	3
The Pacific	Papua New Guinea	1
South Asia	Bangladesh	3
	India	9
Central and West Asia	Pakistan	1
	Tajikistan	1
TOTAL		**13 (unique)**

Source: Authors.

REFERENCES

Abdul Latif Jameel Poverty Action Lab (J-PAL). 2018. Reducing Search Barriers for Job Seekers. *J-PAL Policy Insights.* April.

———. 2023. Vocational and Skills Training Programs to Improve Labor Market Outcomes. *J-PAL Policy Insights.* March.

Abebe, G. et al. 2017. Job Fairs: Matching Firms and Workers in a Field Experiment in Ethiopia. *Policy Research Working Papers.* No. 8092. Washington, DC: World Bank.

Altbeker, A. 2015. Harambee—Youth Employment Accelerator: Case Study from South Africa. Presentation for the Center for International Development at Harvard University Symposium on Inclusive Growth and Development. Cambridge, MA. 9 November.

Andersen, T., L. Feiler, and G. Schulz. 2016. *The Role of Employment Service Providers Guide to Anticipating and Matching Skills and Jobs.* Volume 4. Luxembourg: Publications Office of the European Union.

Apunyo, R. et al. 2022. Interventions to Increase Youth Employment: An Evidence and Gap Map. *Campbell Systemic Reviews.* 18(1). e1216.

Asia-Pacific Economic Cooperation (APEC) Human Resource Working Group. 2019. *Best Practices of Youth Employment Policies in Selected APEC Economies.* Singapore: APEC Secretariat.

Asian Development Bank (ADB). 2018a. *Asian Development Outlook (ADO) 2018: How Technology Affects Jobs.* Manila.

———. 2018b. *Strategy 2030: Achieving a Prosperous, Inclusive, Resilient, and Sustainable Asia and the Pacific.* Manila.

———. 2022a. *Key Indicators for Asia and the Pacific 2022.* Manila.

———. 2022b. *The Social Protection Indicator for Asia: Tracking Developments in Social Protection.* Manila.

———. 2022c. Youth Employment Support in Asia and the Pacific: What Works. *ADB Briefs.* No. 211. Manila.

ADB and International Labour Organization (ILO). 2017. *Improving Labour Market Outcomes in the Pacific: Policy Challenges and Priorities.* Suva: ILO Pacific Office.

———. 2020. *Tackling the COVID-19 Youth Employment Crisis in Asia and the Pacific.* Suva: ILO Pacific Office.

ADB and LinkedIn. 2022. *Digital Jobs and Digital Skills: A Shifting Landscape in Asia and the Pacific.* Manila: ADB.

Association of Southeast Asian Nations (ASEAN). 2021. *Regional Study Report on Human Resources Development Readiness in ASEAN: Regional Report.* Jakarta.

Autor, D. 2009. Introduction to Studies of Labor Market Intermediation. In D. Autor, ed. *Studies of Labor Market Intermediation*. Chicago: University of Chicago Press.

Badan Pusat Statistik (BPS). 2019. *Booklet Survei Angkatan Kerja Nasional Agustus 2019.* Jakarta.

Barbarasa, E., J. Barrett, and N. Goldin. 2017. *Skills Gap or Signaling Gap? Insights from LinkedIn in Emerging Markets of Brazil, India, Indonesia, and South Africa.* Washington, DC and Mountain View, CA: Solutions for Youth Employment and LinkedIn.

Barford, A. and R. Coombe. 2019. *Getting By: Young People's Working Lives.* Cambridge, UK: University of Cambridge.

Bassi, V. and A. Nansamba. 2017. Information Frictions in the Labor Market: Evidence from a Field Experiment in Uganda. *Growth in Labour Markets in Low Income Countries Programme (GLM LIC) Working Papers. No. 29.* Bonn: Institute of Labor Economics (IZA).

BDjobs.com.

Beam, E. A. 2016. Do Job Fairs Matter? Experimental Evidence on the Impact of Job-Fair Attendance. *Journal of Development Economics*. 120. pp. 32–40.

Bell, D. N. and D. G. Blanchflower. 2011. Young People and the Great Recession. *Oxford Review of Economic Policy*. 27(2). pp. 241–267.

Belot, M., P. Kircher, and P. Muller. 2019. Providing Advice to Jobseekers at Low Cost: An Experimental Study on Online Advice. *The Review of Economic Studies.* 86(4). pp. 1411–1447.

Bird, N. and W. Silva. 2020. The Role of Social Protection in Young People's Transition to Work in the Middle East and North Africa (MENA). *International Policy Centre for Inclusive Growth (IPC-IG) Research Reports.* No. 41. Brasília and Amman: IPC-IG and UNICEF Middle East and North Africa Regional Office.

Bobba, M. et al. 2019. Labor Market Search, Informality, and On-the-Job Human Capital Accumulation. *IZA Discussion Papers.* No. 1209. Bonn: IZA.

Briter Bridges. 2020. Digitising the Informal Sector across Underserved Markets. 26 November.

Card, D., J. Kluve, and A. Weber. 2017. What Works? A Meta Analysis of Recent Active Labor Market Program Evaluations. *Journal of the European Economic Association*. 16(3). pp. 894–931.

CareerBuilder. An Introduction to SocialReferral.

Carnevale, A., T. Jayasundera, and D. Repnikov. 2014. *Understanding Online Job Ads Data: A Technical Report.* Washington, DC: Georgetown University, Center on Education and the Workforce, McCourt School of Public Policy.

Carranza, E. et al. 2021. Job Search and Hiring with Two-Sided Limited Information about Workseekers' Skills. *Policy Research Working Papers.* No. 9345. Washington, DC: World Bank.

Causa, O., N. Luu, and M. Abendschein. 2021. Labour Market Transitions across OECD Countries: Stylised Facts. *Economics Department Working Papers.* No. 1692. Paris: Organisation for Economic Co-operation and Development (OECD).

Cebulla, A. and S. Whetton. 2018. All Roads Leading to Rome? The Medium Term Outcomes of Australian Youth's Transition Pathways from Education. *Journal of Youth Studies.* 21(3). pp. 304–323.

Chacaltana, J. and S. Dasgupta, eds. 2021. *Is the Future Ready for Youth? Youth Employment Policies for Evolving Labour Markets.* Geneva: ILO.

Chacaltana, J., S. Elder, and M. Lee. 2019. Youth Transitions and Lifetime Trajectory. *Employment Policy Department Working Papers.* No. 253. Geneva: ILO.

Conlon, J. J. et al. 2018. Labor Market Search with Imperfect Information and Learning. *National Bureau of Economic Research (NBER) Working Papers.* No. 24988. Cambridge, MA: NBER.

Cottier, L. et al. 2018. Does Job Search Assistance Really Raise Employment? *IZA Discussion Papers.* No. 11766. Bonn: IZA.

Datta, N. et al. 2018. Integrated Youth Employment Programs: A Stocktake of Evidence on What Works in Youth Employment Programs. *Jobs Working Papers.* No. 24. Washington, DC: World Bank.

Deen Dayal Upadhyaya Grameen Kaushalya Yojana.

Diamond, P. A. 1982. Aggregate Demand Management in Search Equilibrium. *Journal of Political Economy*. 90(5). pp. 881–894.

Enablecode.

Escudero, V. and E. L. Mourelo. 2015. The Youth Guarantee Programme in Europe: Features, Implementation and Challenges. *Research Department Working Papers.* No. 4. Geneva: ILO.

Eskwelabs.

European Centre for the Development of Vocational Training (Cedefop). 2019. The Online Job Vacancy Market in the EU: Driving Forces and Emerging Trends. *Cedefop Research Papers.* No. 72. Luxembourg: Publications Office of the European Union.

Firstnaukri.com.

Flynn, J., P. Mader, M. Oosterom, and S. Ripoll. 2016. Failing Young People? Addressing the Supply-Side Bias and Individualisation in Youth Employment Programming. *Institute of Development Studies (IDS) Evidence Reports.* No. 216, Brighton: IDS.

Foundation for Young Australians. 2018. *The New Work Reality.* Melbourne.

Fox, L. and U. Kaul. 2017. The Evidence Is In: How Should Youth Employment Programs in Low-Income Countries Be Designed? *Policy Research Working Papers.* No. WPS8500. Washington, DC: World Bank.

Fry, J. and C. Boulton. 2013. Prevalence of Transition Pathways in Australia. *Productivity Commission Staff Working Papers.* Canberra: Government of Australia.

Gardiner, D. and M. Goedhuys. 2020. Youth Aspirations and the Future of Work: A Review of the Literature and Evidence. *ILO Working Papers.* No. 8. Geneva: ILO.

General Assembly. 2020. *Student Outcomes Report: 2020.* Singapore.

Generation.

Generation Unlimited. 2018. *Promising Ideas.* New York: United Nations Children's Fund (UNICEF).

———. 2019. *Strategic Analysis.* New York: UNICEF.

Glints.

Global Business Coalition for Education. 2019. *The 2030 Skills Scorecard: Bridging Business, Education, and the Future of Work.* New York: UNICEF.

Google Cloud. Harambee Youth Employment Accelerator: Solving the Youth Unemployment Challenge.

Government of Australia. Recruitment Methods.

Government of India, Ministry of Labour and Employment, Directorate General of Employment (DGE). Model Career Centre (MCC) and Interlinking of Employment Exchanges.

Government of the Philippines, Philippines Statistics Authority. 2022. *April 2022 Labor Force Survey.* Manila.

Groh, M., D. McKenzie, N. Shammout, and T. Vishwanath. 2015. Testing the Importance of Search Frictions and Matching through a Randomized Experiment in Jordan. *IZA Journal of Labor Economics.* 4(1).

Hall, R. E. and S. Schulhofer-Wohl. 2015. Measuring Job-Finding Rates and Matching Efficiency with Heterogeneous Jobseekers. *NBER Working Papers.* No. 20939. Cambridge, MA: NBER.

Hammond, A. et al. 2018. *Women Wavemakers: Practical Strategies for Recruiting and Retaining Women in Coding Bootcamps.* Washington, DC: World Bank.

Harambee. Harambee.

———. 2021. *Our Vision for Systems Change, 2021–2026.* Johannesburg.

Hayashi, R. and N. Matsuda. 2022. *The Impacts of an Online Job Fair in Bangladesh.* Cambridge, MA: American Economic Association for Randomized Controlled Trials (AEA RCT) Registry.

Heller, S. B. and J. B. Kessler. 2022. Information Frictions and Skill Signaling in the Youth Labor Market. *NBER Working Papers.* No. 29579. Cambridge, MA: NBER.

Hensvik, L., T. Le Barbanchon, and R. Rathelot. 2020. Job Search during the COVID-19 Crisis. *IZA Discussion Papers.* No. 13237. Bonn: IZA.

Honorati, M. and A. Marguerie. 2021. *Youth Employment in Uzbekistan. Opportunities and Challenges.* Washington, DC: World Bank.

Hovhannisyan, S. et al. 2022. Global Job Quality. Evidence from Wage Employment across Developing Countries. *Policy Research Working Papers.* No. 10134. Washington, DC: World Bank.

HRAsia. 2018. Job Seekers in Malaysia and Singapore Prefer to Use Their Mobile to Hunt for Jobs. 12 June.

Huijsmans, R., N. Ansell, and P. Froerer. 2021. Introduction: Development, Young People, and the Social Production of Aspirations. *The European Journal of Development Research.* 33. pp. 1–15.

International Labour Organization (ILO). Statistics on Youth. ILOStat (accessed June 2023).

———. Strategies for Youth Employment. Employment Policy Gateway.

———. 2009. *School-to-Work Transition Survey (STWS): A Methodological Guide.* Geneva.

———. 2016. *Non-Standard Employment around the World: Understanding Challenges, Shaping Prospects.* Geneva.

———. 2018a. *Women and Men in the Informal Economy: A Statistical Picture.* Geneva.

———. 2018b. *Asia-Pacific Employment and Social Outlook 2018: Advancing Decent Work for Sustainable Development.* Bangkok.

———. 2019a. From School to Work: An Analysis of Youth Labour Market Transitions. *Spotlight on Work Statistics.* No. 9. Geneva.

———. 2019b. The Working Poor or How a Job Is No Guarantee of Decent Living Conditions. *Spotlight on Work Statistics.* No. 6. Geneva.

———. 2020a. *Global Employment Trends for Youth 2020: Technology and the Future of Jobs.* Geneva.

———. 2020b. Preventing Exclusion from the Labour Market: Tackling the COVID-19 Youth Employment Crisis. *Policy Briefs.* May. Geneva.

———. 2020c. *Public Employment Services and the Future of Work: Training Manual for the CIS Regional Network for Youth Employment Promotion.* Geneva.

———. 2021a. An Update on the Youth Labour Market Impact of the COVID-19 Crisis. *Statistical Briefs*. June. Geneva.

———. 2021b. *World Employment and Social Outlook 2021: The Role of Digital Labour Platforms in Transforming the World of Work*. Geneva.

———. 2021c. Public employment services that work for young people. Chapter from: Is the future ready for youth?

———. 2022a. *Global Employment Trends for Youth 2022: Investing in Transforming Futures for Young People*. Geneva.

———. 2022b. *Global Report—Technology Adoption in Public Employment Services: Catching up with the Future*. Geneva.

———. 2022c. *Youth Not in Employment, Education or Training in Asia and the Pacific: Trends and Policy Considerations*. Geneva.

International Telecommunication Union (ITU). 2016. *Coding Bootcamps: A Strategy for Youth Employment in Developing Countries*. Geneva.

Iskander, M. and N. Rankin. 2019. We Must Equip Young People to Bounce Back into Work. *Daily Maverick*. 29 October.

JobStart.

Jobtech Alliance. Jobtech Alliance.

Johnson, E. M. et al. 2020. *Increasing Digital Platform Use to Help Youth Find Work*. Research Triangle Park, NC: Research Triangle International (RTI) Press.

Jones, H. 2022. Young People's Schooling Trajectories and Transitions to Social Adulthood in the Context of Brazil's Bolsa Família. *Critical Social Policy*. pp. 1–21.

Karaoglu, G., E. Hargittai, and M. H. Nguyen. 2022. Inequality in Online Job Searching in the Age of Social Media. *Information, Communication and Society*. 25(12). pp. 1826–1844.

Kluve, J. et al. 2017. *Interventions to Improve the Labour Market Outcomes of Youth: A Systematic Review of Training, Entrepreneurship Promotion, Employment Services and Subsidized Employment Interventions*. Oslo: Campbell Collaboration.

Kuhn, P. and H. Mansour. 2011. Is Internet Job Search Still Ineffective? *IZA Discussion Papers*. No. 5955. Bonn: IZA.

Lee, J. W. 2016. How Can Asia Close Its Emerging Skills Gap? World Economic Forum. 15 January.

Lim, C. and A. Grant. 2014. *Unleashing Youth in Asia—Solving for the "Triple-E" Challenge of Youth: Education, Employment and Engagement*. New York: McKinsey and Company.

Loxha, A. and M. Morgandi. 2014. Profiling the Unemployed: A Review of OECD Experiences and Implications for Emerging Economies. *Social Protection and Labor Discussion Papers.* No. SP 1424. Washington, DC: World Bank.

Lyon, S., M. Ranzani, and F. Rosati. 2012. Skill Deficits in Developing Countries: A Review of Empirical Evidence from Enterprise Surveys. Background paper prepared for the Education for All Global Monitoring Report 2012. Paris: United Nations Educational, Scientific and Cultural Organization (UNESCO).

Maroney, J. 2019. Boosting Employee Experience at the Frontline. *Forbes.* 18 November.

Matsumoto, M. and S. Elder. 2010. Characterizing the School-to-Work Transitions of Young Men and Women: Evidence from the ILO School-to-Work Transition Surveys. *Employment Working Papers.* No. 51. Washington, DC: World Bank.

McKinsey Global Institute. 2017. Technology, Jobs, and the Future of Work. Briefing note prepared for the Fortune-Time Global Forum. The Vatican. 3 December 2016.

Mitra, P. P. 2022. Active Labor Market Policies in Developing Asia: Case Study of India. In L. Arthur and D. Hondo, eds. *Strengthening Active Labor Market Policies to Drive an Inclusive Recovery in Asia.* Tokyo: ADB Institute.

Mortensen, D. T. and C. A. Pissarides. 1994. Job Creation and Job Destruction in the Theory of Unemployment. *Review of Economic Studies*. 61(3). pp. 397–415.

Mueller, G. et al. 2022. *Youth in a Time of Crisis: Livelihood Diaries from Nepal and Indonesia during COVID-19*. Cambridge, UK: Restless Development Nepal and University of Cambridge Institute for Sustainability Leadership.

Mulderig, M. C. 2013. An Uncertain Future: Youth Frustration and the Arab Spring. *The Pardee Papers.* No. 16. Boston: Boston University, Frederick S. Pardee Center for the Study of the Longer-Range Future.

O'Higgins, N. 1997. The Challenge of Youth Unemployment. *International Social Security Review.* 50(4). pp. 63–93.

———. 2017. *Rising to the Youth Employment Challenge: New Evidence on Key Policy Issues.* Geneva: ILO.

O'Higgins, N., S. Verick, and A. Elsheikhi. 2021. On the Nature of the Impact of the COVID-19 Pandemic on Youth Labour Markets: A Cross-Country Analysis. Paper prepared for the 7th Conference of the Regulating for Decent Work Network. Geneva. 6–9 July.

Okubo, Y. and K. Sakurai. 2015. Job Seeker Trends 2015: Channels, Search Time, and Income Change. 16 December. Boston: Boston Consulting Group.

Organisation for Economic Co-operation and Development (OECD). 2013. *The OECD Action Plan for Youth: Giving Youth a Better Start in the Labor Market.* Meeting of the OECD Council at Ministerial Level. Paris. 29–30 May.

———. 2015. *Skills for Social Progress: The Power of Social and Emotional Skills.* Paris.

———. 2020a. Employment and Skills Strategies in Indonesia. *OECD Reviews on Local Job Creation.* Paris.

———. 2020b. Public Employment Services in the Frontline for Employees, Jobseekers and Employers. *OECD Policy Responses to Coronavirus (COVID-19).* 28 April. Paris.

———. 2021a. Scaling Up Policies That Connect People with Jobs in the Recovery from COVID-19. *OECD Policy Responses to Coronavirus (COVID-19).* 29 April. Paris.

———. 2021b. *The Updated OECD Youth Action Plan: Building Blocks for Future Action.* Meeting of the Council at Ministerial Level. Paris. 31 May–1 June.

———. 2022a. Delivering for Youth: How Governments Can Put Young People at the Centre of the Recovery. *OECD Policy Responses to Coronavirus (COVID-19).* Paris. 17 March.

———. 2022b. *Education Policy Outlook 2022: Transforming Pathways for Lifelong Learners.* Paris.

———. 2022c. Harnessing Digitalisation in Public Employment Services to Connect People with Jobs. *Policy Briefs on Active Labour Market Policies.* June. Paris.

Padmakanthi, N. P. D. 2022. Effectiveness of Vocational Training Programs in Achieving Decent Work for Youth: The Case of Sri Lanka. In L. Arthur and D. Hondo, eds. *Strengthening Active Labor Market Policies to Drive an Inclusive Recovery in Asia.* Tokyo: ADB Institute.

Palmer, R. 2018. *Jobs and Skills Mismatch in the Informal Economy.* Geneva: ILO.

Pople, A. 2020. The Paradox of Search Frictions in Online Job Matching. *Private Enterprise Development in Low-Income Countries.*

Pritchett, L. 2013. *The Rebirth of Education: Schooling Ain't Learning.* Washington, DC: Center for Global Development.

Sakamoto, A. and J. Sung, eds. 2018. *Skills and the Future of Work: Strategies for Inclusive Growth in Asia and the Pacific.* Geneva: ILO.

Sanderson, E. 2019. Youth Transitions to Employment: Longitudinal Evidence from Marginalised Young People in England. *Journal of Youth Studies.* 23(10). pp. 1310–1329.

Schady, N. et al. 2023. *Collapse and Recovery: How the COVID-19 Pandemic Eroded Human Capital and What to Do about It.* Washington, DC: World Bank.

Schmid, G. 2017. Transitional Labour Markets: Theoretical Foundations and Policy Strategies. In M. Vernengo, E. P. Caldentey, and B. J. Rosser Jr., eds. *The New Palgrave Dictionary of Economics.* London: Palgrave Macmillan.

Singh, S. and Z. Lau. 2020. *S4YE's Impact Portfolio: A Factbook.* Washington, DC: World Bank.

Smith, A. 2015. Searching for Work in the Digital Era. Pew Research Center. 19 November.

Sullivan, P. and T. To. 2011. Search and Non-Wage Job Characteristics. *United States Bureau of Labor Statistics (BLS) Working Papers.* No. 449. Washington, DC: BLS.

United Nations (UN). Goal 8. Sustainable Development.

———. Our Common Agenda.

———. Transforming Education Summit.

———. 2015. *Transforming Our World: The 2030 Agenda for Sustainable Development.* New York.

———. 2018. *The World Youth Report: Youth and the 2030 Agenda for Sustainable Development.* New York.

United Nations Children's Fund (UNICEF). 2019a. More than Half of South Asian Youth Are Not on Track to Have the Education and Skills Necessary for Employment in 2030. News release. 30 October.

———. 2019b. *Transitions from School to Work.* New York.

United Nations Department of Economic and Social Affairs (UNDESA). 2018. Promoting the Inclusion of Young People through Social Protection. *Social Development Briefs.* No. 5. New York.

———. 2019. *World Population Prospects 2019: Highlights.* New York.

United Nations Economic and Social Commission for Asia and the Pacific (UNESCAP). 2022. Promoting Decent Work Opportunities for Older Persons in the Asia-Pacific Region in the Context of the Fourth Industrial Revolution. *Social Development Policy Briefs.* No. 2. Bangkok.

Vaccaro, G. et al. 2022. Measuring Labour Market Transitions Using a Life-Course Perspective in Selected Developed and Developing Countries: An Inventory of Existing Panel Data and Methods of Analysis. *Background Paper Series of the Joint European Union–ILO Project, Building Partnerships on the Future of Work.* No. 4. Geneva: ILO.

Virtualahan.

Wasmer, E. and Y. Zenou. 2005. Equilibrium Search Unemployment with Explicit Spatial Frictions. *IZA Discussion Papers.* No. 1465. Bonn: IZA.

World Bank. Lower Secondary Completion Rate, Total (% of Relevant Age Group)—Asia and the Pacific. Open Data (accessed 28 February 2023).

———. Lower Secondary Completion Rate, Total (% of Relevant Age Group)—South Asia (accessed 28 February 2023).

———. School Enrollment, Tertiary (% Gross)—East Asia and the Pacific. Open Data (accessed 23 May 2023).

———. School Enrollment, Tertiary (% Gross)—South Asia. Open Data (accessed 23 May 2023).

———. Skills Development.

———. World Development Indicators (accessed June 2023).

———. 2006. *World Development Report 2007: Development and the Next Generation.* Washington, DC.

———. 2012. *World Development Report 2013: Jobs.* Washington, DC.

———. 2017. *Jobless Growth? South Asia Economic Focus 2018.* Washington, DC.

———. 2020. *International Development Association Project Appraisal Document on a Proposed Credit in the Amount of SDR25.5 Million (US$35 Million Equivalent) to the Independent State of Papua New Guinea for an Urban Youth Employment Project II.* Washington, DC.

World Economic Forum (WEF). 2020. *Jobs of Tomorrow: Mapping Opportunity in the New Economy.* Geneva.

WEF and National University of Singapore. 2022. *Future Readiness of SMEs and Mid-Sized Companies: A Year On.* Geneva: WEF.

Yashif, E. 2007. Labor Search and Matching in Macroeconomics. *IZA Discussion Papers.* No. 2743. Bonn: IZA.

Yeyati, E. L., M. Montane, and L. Sartorio. 2019. What Works for Active Labor Market Policies? *Center for International Development Working Papers.* No. 358. Cambridge, MA: Harvard University.

Youth Co:Lab. 2021. *How Young Entrepreneurs in Asia-Pacific Responded to COVID-19.* New York: United Nations Development Programme.

Youth Policy Labs. Global Youth Policy Reviews.

www.ingramcontent.com/pod-product-compliance
Lightning Source LLC
Chambersburg PA
CBHW041756220926
51847CB00014B/225
9789292704018